GOD MY EXCEEDING JOY

God
My Exceeding Joy

By

AMOS LUNDQUIST

AUGUSTANA PRESS

ROCK ISLAND, ILLINOIS

GOD MY EXCEEDING JOY

⎡ PRINTED ⎤
⎣ IN U·S·A· ⎦

AUGUSTANA BOOK CONCERN
Printers and Binders
ROCK ISLAND, ILLINOIS
1956

To my Wife, Ruth

To him who loves us and has freed us from our sins by his blood and made us a kingdom, priests to his God and Father, to him be glory and dominion for ever and ever. Amen. Revelation 1: 5, 6.

Acknowledgments

Bible quotations are from the Revised Standard Version of the Bible, Copyright, 1946 and 1952, by Division of Christian Education of the National Council of the Churches of Christ in America, and are used by permission.

Zondervan Publishing House, Grand Rapids, Michigan, for permission to use material from the author's previous book, *The Secret of Spiritual Victory.*

Mrs. Joseph Fort Newton for permission to use certain illustrations from the writings of her late husband.

Houghton Mifflin Company, for use of quotation from *The Life of Alice Freeman Palmer* by George Herbert Palmer.

A. L.

Other books by Pastor Lundquist

Better Choir Singing

Inspirational Readings

The Secret of Spiritual Victory

Inspiration for Today

Lives that Glorify God

Contents

Chapter I

WHEN A MAN COMES TO HIMSELF

WE have a new daddy at our house," exclaimed the children. "Something has happened to our old daddy. He feels so much better, and now he treats us like a real daddy ought to treat his children."

"What has happened to Mr. Jones?" inquired his fellow workmen. "He's a new man altogether. He seems so happy, and he's ever so much more congenial."

"What a gentleman Mr. Jones has become lately," said one of his neighbors to another. "There has been such a great improvement in his personality. Lately he seems so contented, and now he is a real neighbor."

A young lady who lived under adverse home conditions became so mentally distressed that her sadness was reflected in her face and in her voice, and spoiled everything she tried to do. Some time later something deeply helpful happened to her. Her attitude was altogether transformed. Seeing her smiling face a friend inquired, "How are things at home? Have they changed for the better?" "No," the young lady replied. "Things are just the same as ever; but I have changed."

Someone asked Dr. Daniel A. Poling what actual good he had gotten out of his knowledge of God. Replied Dr. Poling, "I do not know much about God or Christianity, but what I do know has changed my life."

So great has been the change in the lives of countless people through the incoming and indwelling of a new spirit that in ages past some people have happily adopted new names, such as Newman, Neumann, Nyman, or Neander. In each case the new name testifies that there is a new man.

Every day and every hour, somewhere, somebody is discovering and accepting for himself this new life in Christ. What God has done and is doing with innumerable others, He is well able and willing to do for any one of us who may hunger and yearn for something better than we now experience.

Without Christ, life is chaos. Even at its best, the physical life is not the real life, for without a second birth man lives only a fractional existence. It is only when the Spirit of God moves upon the firmament of man's soul, and a person begins to heed the call of God, that he really begins to live. Christianity is essentially a new creation, a new race, a new family.

One night Nicodemus, a teacher in Israel, came to Christ. Outwardly he was a good man, and wise in the things of the world. But with all his learning and wide experience in teaching others, there remained in his own heart a great void. He might deceive others about his real spiritual condition, but he could not outwit himself, nor could he hoodwink his Creator.

In all the literature available to him, Nicodemus could find nothing spiritually satisfying or personally applicable. In the lives and the attitudes of his fellow men he found few, if any, who really walked with God.

Languishing in the chilling shadows of earth, Nicodemus yearned to breathe afresh the free, God-kissed air of eternity. How he longed to be living the best life possible! How much he desired to lay hold of God himself, or rather, wanted God to lay hold on him! How he craved to see God and to hear God in some burning bush! To walk with God,

2

like Enoch of old, was his sincere ambition. He wanted really to be alive.

For a long time Nicodemus had studied religion. He had taught it to others. But even though he had tried to make his teaching simple, understandable, and helpful to the everyday experiences of others, somehow he never discovered the secret of inner personal joy and peace. To have his religious vision corrected, he came to Christ. He wanted his sense of religious values stabilized. Lost in the wilderness of life, he wisely took time to determine his spiritual bearings.

In blending his numerous paints, an artist sometimes becomes confused and loses his sense of true primary colors. Then he has to stop and inspect color charts or gems. In like manner Nicodemus was wise in stopping to ascertain the things that truly belong to the Spirit of God.

When a person is in a boat on a lake or river or ocean, he looks for assurance of safe direction by checking his position in relation to some permanent object on the shore, or in the sky, or to the magnetic pole. If the weather turns stormy and the boat begins to pitch and to roll, he can retain his health and composure much longer if he will keep looking off to the horizon which remains level and quiet and steady. In order to determine the position of some stationary point the navigator of a ship at sea uses binoculars, or a lead line, or compass, or sextant, or radio, or radar, or sonar, or whatever may be available. Sometimes only ordinary eyesight is sufficient.

In a spiritual way Nicodemus wanted to be sure of his position, his direction, and his progress as far as eternal values were concerned. Threatened by world-sickness, he wanted to look off to a safe and solid "horizon." Lost in the fog of inadequate information, unsatisfying experience, and

3

spiritual bewilderment, he wanted to discover and to use any means at all available to guide him safely to his God-intended home port.

Nicodemus was willing to try anything at all which Jesus might suggest in order that he might enjoy a fresh revelation of God. He was eager, if necessary, to discard all human and preconceived notions of religion, if only he might come to assurance that God really loved him and held him in His strong, everlasting arms, so that he might find rest for his soul.

Nicodemus wanted to feel the invigorating lifeblood from the Eternal Heart coursing through his own anemic spiritual arteries. He longed to lay his weary ear hard upon the breast of God to become assured of the constant and eternal pulsing of the personal love and the deep wisdom of God.

Prepared to ask many practical questions, Nicodemus came to Jesus. He recognized that Christ possessed a spirit and lived a life that were unquestionably far superior to his own. Nicodemus realized that his own heart and life were such a dismal failure and such a deep disappointment to himself. Only a person like Christ would be able to help him find the spiritual north star and the true and safe magnetic pole of his life. In Christ he was assured that he had found a genuine spiritual Friend who could understand him, inspire him, and help him.

The Lord was not satisfied to give Nicodemus a few spiritual pills or to recommend a few more outward works whereby he might gain favor with God. Jesus cut through Nicodemus' complimentary introduction and told him point blank, "Unless one is born anew he cannot see the kingdom of God." "You must be born anew." A new heart is needed, and a new life.

"How can a man be born when he is old?" asked Nicodemus. He was perplexed, confused, and embarrassed. Learned man that he was, he yet could not understand the divine process of becoming a child of God.

Jesus wanted Nicodemus to believe in God as his spiritual Father. Only God can give life. Only God can sustain or restore life. Only God can be the Father of anyone's spiritual life. The Father of all His true children is God. Children of men cannot create themselves, and children of God cannot create, or redeem, or regenerate, themselves. Nor is the natural man able to transform himself into a new creature in Christ.

Even as a corpse is unable to raise itself to life and activity, so neither can an unsaved person help God in the transformation and renewal of his heart and soul. Man is no creator alongside God. Man is no Savior alongside Christ. It is God who has *begun* the good work in us.

Spiritual renewal is God's work. We are God's workmanship, the garden of God. And most of the work in a garden is God's work, done ever so quietly but effectively. "This is the work of God, that you believe." This is the work of God, that we *live*. The healing of the soul, as well as of the body and of the mind, is God's work.

The source of our life in Jesus Christ is God. Our relation to God is somewhat similar to that of a number of freight or passenger cars to the Diesel locomotive. In themselves the train cars do not have the power to move forward or upward, or to transport their load. If the brakes were released, the cars would roll downward and come to rest at the lowest point of the track.

It is only as the Diesel locomotive is effectively coupled to the cars that the cars can move forward and arrive at

5

their proper destination. The coupler cannot move the train. Only the locomotive can move the train, but the cars must be attached to the locomotive by the coupler. The Diesel locomotive is the abounding grace of God; the coupler is our faith in God. Only God can empower us, and this He does when we are firmly attached to Him by the faith God gives us in himself.

What is effective is not faith in itself, but the righteousness of Jesus Christ which faith grasps and appropriates. The peace of the soul is not derived from contemplating our faith, but from Christ who is our peace.

A man cannot even desire to live the new life until God puts that desire into his heart. It is God who takes the initiative in man's salvation. The author of our salvation is God. God must work all good within us. Man would be wise in learning to be still, to pray for grace to cease resisting the work of God in his heart, and to permit God to do with him anything that He sees needs to be done.

A person does not need to try to live; of course not. Nor does a person need to try to be a son or daughter of his own parents. In like manner a person need not *try* to be a Christian or a child of God. This is God's work. How thankful we ought to be for what God already has done for us and in us! Are we not wise, then, for our own sakes and for our own good, in welcoming the unassisted work of God in our hearts and lives!

In Christian experience it does no good for man to try to lift himself up to God. Christianity reveals that in love God reaches down to transform and renew human hearts and lives. Before man ever seeks God, God is seeking him. Before man ever channels his television to God, God has been operating His own powerful transmitting station, sending forth His far-reaching and personal gospel of spiritual adjustment and opportunity. If a person has the least yearn-

6

ing for God, God has already started His work of grace in that person's life.

God desires to bring about a restoration of His own image in human life. In every heart God wants to create a genuine love of truth, a delight in beauty, a passion for justice, and a willingness to exchange things of temporary value for blessings of lasting value.

How thankful the children of God should be for what He has already done for them in bringing about a renewal of spiritual living! Already God is feeding and strengthening the new life. Every day in some way God is perfecting our faith in Him. He permits various experiences to come into the lives of His children, so that they are given the opportunity to be drawn ever closer to Him through Bible study and prayer. In such a manner the new life may be nourished, strengthened, and perfected.

Jesus said that it was because of the Father that He lived. "I live because of the Father." And sooner or later every child of God will say the same.

It was the love of the father that eventually brought the prodigal son home again. After the son came home, the father said, "my son was dead, and is alive again." The father's love had created a new heart in his son, and from then on the son appreciated his father more than ever before.

In his later life Peter wrote concerning his own spiritual rebirth, "Blessed be the God and Father of our Lord Jesus Christ! By his great mercy we have been born anew to a living hope through the resurrection of Jesus Christ from the dead." It was the resurrection of Jesus which God used to arouse Peter's dormant soul into spiritual alertness and vigor.

Paul once wrote to his friends, "Even when we were dead through our trespasses, (God) made us alive together with

Christ." He also said, "He (God) destined us in love to be his sons through Jesus Christ."

Speaking of the new birth, John, the beloved disciple, declared, "But to all who received him, who believed in his name, he gave power to become children of God; who were born, not of blood nor of the will of the flesh nor of the will of man, but of God."

More beautiful than the creation of a lovely flower, more impressive than the creation of a mighty mountain, is the glorious work of God in the conversion and spiritual awakening of a single soul. Day by day God comes to us and offers himself to us in order that we may be truly alive to our spiritual opportunities.

Jesus reminded Nicodemus of the time when the Israelites rebelled against God and against Moses, and God sent serpents among the people. Then God commanded Moses to make a brazen serpent to which the people could look in faith and be healed. Christ suggested that if Nicodemus would look to God's love for the world, to God's love for anyone at all, to God's love for Nicodemus, he would be healed and saved. Nicodemus looked to God, and found life eternal.

When Adam and Eve sinned they were driven out of the garden of Eden. Nevermore could they go back to the garden. Their children could not return, nor their grandchildren. Humanity has never been able to go back. Because of the sin of Adam and Eve all are under the curse. All have lost the image of God.

But in Christ, God offers to restore to His penitent and trusting children His own image and to bring believers back into His good graces again.

The only real Son that God has is Jesus. All other children of God are adopted children. When a child is to be adopted, the new parents, after a six months' or a year's

8

probation, go before a certain judge. He advises the new parents that they are to treat the child as their own, to love him, to provide all that is necessary for him, to give him their own last name, and to see to it that the child receives just as much inheritance as though he were their own.

In the same manner when a child or a person is baptized in the name of the Triune God and accepts Christ as his personal Savior, God adopts him and accepts him as His own. God promises to provide for him, to give him a home, to love him, to give him His own name, and to give him as much inheritance as He would to His own Son. How can a Christian comprehend all that is involved in God's adopting any of us as His children?

When a child is adopted into a family it becomes quite important in due time that the child also adopts and accepts his new parents. In most instances he learns to respond to their love for him; he begins to love his new father and mother and to accept them as his own. He trusts them to provide for him as long as it is necessary.

In like manner a baptized believer in due time learns to adopt and to accept his heavenly Father as his own. He begins to trust Him for time and for eternity. Let no one rebel against his new Father! Rather, it is far better for each believer to appreciate all that his new Father has done for him in the past and wants to do for him in the immediate future, and forever. What a boundless opportunity and privilege God offers to His baptized and adopted children!

The home of one of our pastors had a son whom the parents loved very much. Then they adopted a baby girl. They loved her also. Some twenty years later someone inquired from the parents, "Do you see any difference between your love for your own son and for your adopted daughter?" "No," replied the father, "we see no difference at all. We love our adopted daughter just as much as we love our own son."

Is it not true also of God's love for His adopted children? Surely He loves His adopted children as much as He loves His own Son. God not only provides for all His children in this life. He is also planning to share a significant inheritance, not only with His own Son, but with all His adopted children as well.

> *All that I was, my sin, my guilt,*
> *My death, was all my own;*
> *All that I am, I owe to Thee,*
> *My gracious God, alone.*

HORATIUS BONAR.

10

Chapter II

HOW LIFE WITH CHRIST BEGINS

ONE day Tennyson went walking in a garden with a friend of his. The friend was not a Christian, but evidently was a seeker. Turning to Tennyson the friend inquired, "Alfred, I cannot believe in your religion, but I do believe in you. What does Jesus really mean to you?"

After a moment's reflection Tennyson pointed to a rose growing in the garden and declared, "I will tell you. What the sun in the sky means to this flower, giving it life, beauty and fragrance, that is what Jesus Christ means to my life."

A seminary president once said, "So much modern faith is only historical. It knows about Jesus, but it doesn't know Jesus. To such faith, Jesus was; to real faith, Jesus is. Is Jesus real to me? We are on quest for reality in religion. At least, folks on many a hand are beginning to see a new vision of Jesus as He really is.

"There isn't any point in any person's doing anything for Christ until he first lets Christ do something fundamental for him. Jesus' presence makes all the difference in the world. Without Jesus' presence in my heart, my highest wisdom is futile. Without Jesus' presence in my heart, my strength is nothing but weakness. But Jesus does live in my heart, and He empowers me, so I need fear nothing at all."

"Until we see Calvary," said one of our pastors, "we cannot see Christ." Christ shows himself best on the cross. There all the love, mercy, and grace, of God are concen-

11

trated in the prayers, the testimony, the suffering, and the dying of Christ.

But we go on to see the power of Christ's resurrection at work in our own day. The resurrection of Christ makes all the difference in the lives of His disciples today. The power of Jesus' resurrection is with us even now, for it is Christ who works in us and gives us newness of life.

When Christ was speaking with Nicodemus, He pointed to himself as the Savior of men, "Whoever believes in him should not perish but have eternal life." Whatever God does with His people is done on account of Christ and through Christ. No one comes to the Father except through Christ.

Christ did not come to give us physical life, for this we already have. Christ came to give us a new life, a spiritual life. Christ is the Vine from whom we, His branches, receive life, strength and fruitage. "And this is the testimony, that God gave us eternal life, and this life is in his Son."

At another time our Lord said, "He who believes in the Son has eternal life." He who looks trustingly to the Christ of Calvary, willing to believe in His finished work of redemption, has eternal life. He who believes has, possesses, is living, the life eternal. "Has" is present time, and refers to present time, to all time, even to timelessness. He who now believes in Christ now has eternal life. He who now believes is now living the life that never ends. Somewhat in kind, although not in degree, he is living like Christ lived in Palestine.

The Savior declared that He came in order that His followers "may have life and have it abundantly." He also asserted, "Because I live, you will live also." To Martha He said, "I am the resurrection and the life; he who believes in me, though he die, yet shall he live, and whoever lives and believes in me shall never die."

12

In the conclusion of his gospel the beloved disciple John wrote, "But these are written that you may believe that Jesus is the Christ, the Son of God, and that believing you may have life in his name." And in one of his epistles John says, "I write this to you who believe in the name of the Son of God, that you may know that you have eternal life." He also stated, "He who has the Son has life."

One day our Lord was invited to the little home in Bethany. Martha, as was her custom, served. Mary sat and listened to her Lord. But the most awed person in the group was Lazarus who had been raised from the dead. It was because of Christ that Lazarus was alive. How Lazarus must have looked at Jesus! How he listened to every word of Christ with a worshipful heart!

It was because of Jesus' presence, prayer, and power that Lazarus again was alive. It was because of Christ that Lazarus could again walk the streets of his village, that he could attend the synagogue and visit the temple, that he could go about his daily work, that he could sit there at the table and enjoy the good fellowship.

So it is with all who have experienced the life-giving love of Christ. If it were not for Christ we should be dead in our trespasses and sins. But because of Jesus' presence, prayer, and power, we are spiritually alive today. Thank God for that! Because of His saving grace, and His coming to us in His Word, we today can walk the streets, we can attend church, we can go about our daily work with new zest, we can enjoy sweet fellowship with Him and with His people.

What happened to Barabbas? As we recall, Barabbas was imprisoned for murder, robbery and insurrection. Obviously he was a bad man. But at the trial of Jesus the mob demanded the crucifixion of our Lord and called for the release of Barabbas. Barabbas thus became free to walk the streets again.

What should Barabbas now do with his new freedom? Should he continue associating with bad characters? Should he devote his life to crime? Was he so ungrateful to this Stranger from Galilee who died in his place that he would continue in a life of sin?

We do not know what happened to Barabbas. Certainly he should have stopped to think for a minute that Christ took his place and died. Barabbas should have spent the remainder of his life witnessing to what Christ had done for him.

In like manner, it is because of Christ's dying that we are alive today. If Christ had not died, each of us would certainly have died in sin long ago. We all are living on extended time, on resurrected time, so to speak. How can any of us live only for ourselves, when Christ died for others, for each of us? If we would only stop a moment to think, we should begin to appreciate the rare privilege of witnessing to what the death and the resurrection of Christ mean in our own daily life.

Christ is more than a teacher sent from God. Christ is the Life-Giver, sent from God. Jesus could not teach Nicodemus how to receive the new life in God. Christ simply offered himself to Nicodemus, henceforth to live out His own life in and through him, to dwell in him, to think and to speak through him.

The new life in Christ is an exchange; the supremacy of the old life is exchanged for the supremacy of the new life in Christ. Converted Paul said, "It is no longer I who live, but Christ who lives in me." It is Christ for you who is the Savior of men. It is Christ in you who is the hope of glory. It is Christ within that comprises the new nature in the believer.

14

In reality, a converted man has two natures, for the old wayward nature lives along with the new nature. The old nature is still weak and subject to pride and all the marks of human flesh. The new nature, Christ within, seeks to do God's will. All through life these two wage a daily battle. Daily the experience of a Christian is that of sin and grace. Blessed is he who earnestly prays and permits Christ to be victorious in his life daily. Then in truth he will be living a Christian life.

St. Paul said, "Christ is our life," and "For me to live is Christ." To young Titus he wrote, "He *(Christ)* saved us . . . . in virtue of his own mercy, by the washing of regeneration and renewal in the Holy Spirit, which he poured out upon us richly through Jesus Christ our Savior."

Christ is planning a better life for us than anything we have ever thought possible, or desired. He is more ambitious for our lives, in a noble and unselfish way, than we can ever be without His help. He is likewise planning a better life for our family, our friends, as well as for all others, than either we or they can ever imagine. He wants to come and help us do that which we alone can never do. When Christ is permitted to enter the human heart He brings with Him all the grace and power necessary to enable that person to live a real Christian life.

How can the wires of a piano become aware of the beautiful tones and melodies hidden in the inspired mind of the composer? Without the musician a piano is dead. But under his trained fingers it comes to life. It is when someone plays the keys with true understanding of the laws of musical harmony that the piano fulfills its intended purpose. When Christ is permitted to come and play in the human heart the chords of spiritual harmony, a person begins to live as God eternally intended that he should live.

15

A good verse to study is Isaiah 53:6: "All we like sheep have gone astray; we have turned every one to his own way; and the Lord has laid on him the iniquity of us all."

The first half of this verse shows us our need of salvation. Time and again we have strayed away from God's loving purposes for us all. In imagination, in desire, in word, and in deed, we have strayed away from Him. What God has wanted us to do, that we have neglected. What He has wanted us not to do, that we have done. Truly, we have turned every one to his own way. In other words, we are lost sinners!

But the second part of the verse tells us the provision God has made for our salvation. "The Lord has laid on him the iniquity of us all."

Who is it upon whom God has laid my iniquity? It is Jesus.

What, then, has God done with my sin? He has laid my sin on Jesus.

Is it, then, any longer on me? No, not on me.

Where is my sin, then? My sin is on Jesus.

Let us illustrate. My left hand is myself, and my right hand is Christ. First, I lay a heavy book on my left hand, then another book, and another. The load is heavy, and, as time goes on it seems ever heavier. These books represent my sin. Sin is burdensome, and with the passage of time the guilt becomes very heavy, excruciatingly heavy.

But Isaiah says that the Lord has laid on Jesus the iniquity of *us all.*

Then I transfer the heavy books from my left hand to my right hand. Where is now my burden? On my right hand! Where is now my sin? On Jesus, of course!

Are the books any longer on my left hand? No!

16

Is my sin any longer on myself? No, not on me!

Where is my sin? My sin is on Jesus! All my sin, past, present, and future, as well as the iniquity of my depraved heart, Jesus bore on the cross for me.

My all-sufficient Savior is Christ, and this verse tells me so. All I need to do is to accept and confess what God has done for me in Christ. What we need to do is to quit trying, and to start trusting, trusting Christ's finished work of redemption on Calvary.

We need not trust our feelings. We trust God's own Word. If I should put my left hand into very warm water and my right hand into very cold water, one hand would get quite warm, the other quite cold. If, then, I should put both hands in room-temperature water the hand that had been hot would feel cold. The hand that had been cold would feel warm. Neither hand would feel the truth; neither hand would tell the truth. So, what God's word says about us is more dependable than our feelings.

As summer advances into autumn, green leaves on the trees turn to gold, or red, or brown. One by one most of the leaves flutter to the ground, and the bare branches stand silhouetted against the sky.

But on certain oak trees some leaves remain on the twigs all winter long. Frost and biting cold chill and freeze. From the north blustery winds of succeeding blizzards swirl furiously. Occasional breezes from the south and sunshiny days suggest the coming of balmy spring. But in spite of every change of winter weather, in spite of alternating blizzard and thaw, in spite of snow or sunshine, those few leaves cling stubbornly to the twigs all winter long. Not until real spring arrives and the new life-giving sap begins to flow freely upward into all the twigs do these last remaining leaves flutter to the ground.

In the ordinary, on-going experiences of many a Christian

some bad habits are broken, or changed, and transformed into better habits. Time changes many things. As a person learns from the Word of God, the years surprisingly mellow many a difficult life.

In the life of many, some few habits seem to cling with stubborn tenacity throughout the years. Harsh winds of adversity, or accident, or illness, or the frost of serious difficulties, may threaten one's very life. Enticing breezes of occasional prosperity or the sunshine of good fortune may encourage a person at last to yield himself to the better life. But in spite of varying experiences some habits continue.

When a person begins to look into, and study, and make room for, the new life in Christ, then Christ brings with himself power to transform, willingness to accept this new and better viewpoint, and grace to live the new life. Christ brings with Him power to go the right direction, power to let go and to let God lead, power to give up the good and the better for that which is best of all.

When the new life in Christ is permitted to enter, with increasing grace and strength, into a person's inmost soul then things really begin to happen. The impossible becomes possible. The new throws off the old. Good displaces evil. God in His strength overcomes our weakness. The right direction more than replaces the wrong. Sadness is transformed into joy. Disobedience is overwhelmed by the act of obedience. Stubbornness is consecrated into faithfulness. Self-will surrenders to Christ's will. What has happened to the old ways? They are gone. Like the leaves of the oak tree in full springtime, the old ways have dropped away in the rapturous enjoyment of the new life in Christ.

When a person is baptized in the name of the Father, he is also baptized in the name of the Son. He comes into a new relationship with God's Son, our Lord Christ. Certainly Christ accepts, loves, and adopts us as His new brothers and sisters. He seeks to make us feel at home in the new family relationship. As adopted brothers and sisters of Christ, we also should seek to adapt ourselves to Him and to His wishes, and to love and to accept Him as our Elder Brother. As we learn to know Him ever better, we cannot help but sound abroad His well-deserved praises.

An organist was practicing one day on his pipe organ when an insignificant looking stranger walked over to the console and inquired if he might be permitted to play the organ for a few minutes. The organist explained that only a qualified musician would be permitted to play the great organ.

The stranger kept insisting that he would appreciate to play the organ, so at length the organist reluctantly granted permission. What marvelous music echoed through the arches of the great cathedral! The organist sat thrilled.

When the stranger had finished playing, the organist inquired, "Who are you who can play like that?" With simple modesty the stranger replied, "I am Felix Mendelssohn." The organist struck himself on the brow and exclaimed, "Felix Mendelssohn! The master! Almost I did not let the master have his way!"

Almost we do not let the Master have His way!

> *Just as I am, poor, wretched, blind;*
> *Sight, riches, healing of the mind,*
> *Yea, all I need in Thee I find,*
> *O Lamb of God, I come, I come!*

CHARLOTTE ELLIOTT.

Chapter III

HOW THE HOLY SPIRIT WORKS

TO NICODEMUS Jesus said, "That which is born of the Spirit is spirit." Only he who is born of the Spirit is spiritual. A twice-born man is a spiritually-minded man. Our Lord said, "It is the Spirit who gives life." Paul wrote, "To set the mind on the Spirit is life and peace."

In contrast Jesus also said, "That which is born of the flesh is flesh." That is all it is, or ever will be—flesh. It may be educated flesh, or wealthy, or honored. It may be flesh that has performed good works, or is moral, or ritualistic, or long-lived. But it is only flesh, and when death comes, it will perish, and rightly so. "Flesh and blood cannot inherit the Kingdom of God."

To be willing to follow the guidance of the Holy Spirit is to be filled with the life which flows out from God. He who is led by the Spirit of God is a child of God. He who sows to the Spirit, that is, he who invests his life in spiritual values, shall of the Spirit reap life eternal.

It may be that Jesus' words about the Spirit reminded Nicodemus of the words of Ezekiel. A valley was full of bones, "and they were very dry." By their own power they could not possibly live again. But God said to the prophet, "Prophesy to these bones, and say to them, O dry bones, hear the word of the Lord. Thus says the Lord God to these bones, Behold, I will cause breath to enter you, and you shall live."

As he was commanded, Ezekiel prophesied, and even as

he was speaking, he heard a noise, and felt a shaking, and the bones came together joint to joint. Then sinews and flesh came upon the bones, and skin covered them; but there was no breath in them. Through the prophet, God commanded the four winds to come and to blow over the lifeless bodies, and "breath came into them, and they lived, and stood upon their feet, an exceedingly great host . . . Thus says the Lord God: . . . And I will put my Spirit within you, and you shall live."

It is when we let the Spirit of God blow over and into us that we as individuals, families, congregations, institutions, communities, denominations, or nations, shall begin to live. At all times God stands ready to blow His Spirit over and into many a yearning Nicodemus, in order that he might rise, and live, and march as a living witness in the on-going work of Christ.

RECOGNIZING THE HOLY SPIRIT

Speaking of the work of the Holy Spirit in saving lives, Dr. H. E. Dana once said, "Surely psychological processes may be traced in regeneration, but the Holy Spirit is nevertheless the dynamic cause. Have we any factual reason for believing that the Holy Spirit is the originating factor in Christian regeneration? Yes, for when the Holy Spirit's part is repudiated the typical experience cannot be reproduced."

It is a common experience that people who depend alone upon psychological approaches never produce the moral and social results found in true Christian living. When the Holy Spirit is ignored, He cannot work. It is only when the Holy Spirit is implored and permitted to lead, that He produces results.

In explaining the Third Article of the Apostles' Creed, Martin Luther says:

21

"I believe that I cannot by my own reason or strength believe in Jesus Christ my Lord, or come to Him;

but the Holy Spirit has called me through the gospel, enlightened me by His gifts, and sanctified and preserved me in the truth faith;

in like manner as He calls, gathers, enlightens, and sanctifies the whole Christian Church on earth, and preserves it in union with Jesus Christ in the one true faith;

in which Christian Church He daily forgives abundantly all my sins, and the sins of all believers,

and will raise up me and all the dead at the last day,

and will grant everlasting life to me and to all who believe in Christ.

This is most certainly true."

For quite some time the disciples of Christ were only average pupils in the school of the Spirit. Christ had many things to tell them, but some of His disciples were preoccupied with personal affairs, and were only partially alert to His spiritual appeals and challenges. But in time their Teacher, Savior, and Life-giver was taken away from them, crucified, buried, resurrected, and ascended. Then the fearful disciples remained in Jerusalem, gathering together for ten days of intensive prayer and study of the Scriptures. They were mindful also of what Jesus had said to them.

Not only did something happen to Jesus at Jerusalem, but something also happened to the disciples. They passed through the most vital spiritual crisis that men can experience. Remembering the sinless goodness of their Lord, they discovered the deep and terrific depravity of their own hearts and lives. As they encountered the forces of vicious evil and stubborn unbelief, they confessed their own sad helplessness and lack of spiritual vitality.

As they earnestly searched their own lives, the Lord opened their hearts to believe the gospel. At Pentecost the

Lord was pleased to send upon them the outpouring of the Holy Spirit. Then they began to live as true disciples of Christ. They were made wholeheartedly receptive to the Word of Christ, to which they once had not paid close attention. By the indwelling Spirit their lives became transformed; they were born anew.

Their spiritual coolness was now replaced by the glowing tongues of fire. In their daily experience of bringing others to Christ, their own sense of spiritual values was clarified and enhanced. Being led by the Spirit, they became eagerly willing to go any place, to say anything, and to do anything, that would further the growth of the Kingdom of God.

The Holy Spirit Uses the Word of God

A true Christian experience does not come down haphazardly out of the sky. It comes only in the divinely appointed method—through the Word of God. Directly or indirectly, the Spirit operates through the revealed Word of God. There is no genuine re-birth outside of vital contact with that revealed Word. Only God Triune, working through His own Word, can bring spiritual vitality to human life.

In the days of King Josiah, finding the law of God in the temple brought about a spiritual awakening. It was the Word of God spoken by Christ that aroused new life in the hearts of those with whom He came into contact. It was the proclamation of the Word of God that stirred up spiritual awakenings in the days of Luther, Calvin, Wesley, Moody, and others.

In the first temptation our Lord answered the tempter in these words, "Man shall not live by bread alone, but by every word that proceeds from the mouth of God." He also affirmed: . . . "he who hears my word and believes him

23

who sent me, has eternal life; he does not come into judgment, but has passed from death to life."

Paul wrote to Timothy: "Our Savior Christ Jesus . . . brought life and immortality to light through the gospel." He told the Corinthians, "I become your father in Christ Jesus through the gospel." Peter said that true Christians "are born anew . . . through the living and abiding word of God."

People are eagerly studying all kinds of literature in an attempt to reconstruct the human race. They busy themselves with lessons in science, psychology, psychiatry, government, education, economics, militarism, conservation, and so forth, all of which have their proper place. But with all these studies and with all modern conveniences, comforts, and speed, man himself is not necessarily any better.

There can be no genuine permanent improvement until people look to the Christ of the gospels for a new creation in their own hearts. Nothing less than a regeneration of the individual can bring a person into right relations with himself, his God, and his fellow men. All human devices are failing. Only the Holy Spirit, working through the gospel of Christ, can reconstruct the human heart and make all things new. Only the gospel can make a new life, a new city, a new earth, and new heavens.

Lew Wallace intended to study the Bible to prove that Jesus never lived, and that His alleged teachings were only a hoax. But as he read the gospels critically he became convinced that Christ really had lived. He began to realize that what Jesus said made real sense. He began to love Christ and to desire to become a real Christian. Thus God used His own Word to create a new life in the heart and soul of Wallace; and instead of writing a book against Christ, Wallace wrote *Ben Hur* which *glorifies* Christ.

The Word of God was written by the inspiration of the

24

Holy Spirit. Men, "moved by the Holy Spirit," spoke and wrote from God. When a person wants to receive the full power of the written or spoken Word today, he will wisely seek the help of the Holy Spirit. The real key to the Scriptures is the Holy Spirit. Without the Holy Spirit the Bible could not have been written. Without the Holy Spirit the Bible today cannot rightly be read or heard.

Nicodemus did not pretend that he was better than he really was. He permitted the Holy Spirit to enlighten him; he listened attentively to the gospel which Christ spoke to him. He was thankful that God had already created new life in his soul. In faith he looked to Christ as his Savior, and did not perish, but had life eternal.

And now, being born anew, Nicodemus soon learned that something definite had happened to him. He was a new creature in Christ. He belonged to Christ's second creation. He was experiencing "newness of life." And this newness of life was manifested by a newness of direction, a new conscience, a new will, a new mind, a new ambition, a new love, a new devotion, a new source of sustenance, a new attitude, a new goal, and a new Master.

He who is born of the Spirit is born, not for self, but for God. His goal is outward, upward, and heavenward. Now he is a beloved child of God, an heir of the Father, a joint heir with Christ. A God-given peace bestows upon him a foretaste of the glories of the ultimate crown of life.

Dr. C. B. Gohdes relates that a father and his son had gone to services on Whitsunday and listened attentively to the sermon. Impressed with what had been said, the son afterward asked the father, "Father, what is the difference between a man who has received the Holy Spirit and one who has not?"

"The difference," replied the father, "between one who has received the Holy Spirit and one who has not is the difference between a needle which has been brought into the field of a strong electrical current and becomes magnetized and one that is only passive and not subject to magnetic influence. The magnetic needle has hidden powers. In darkness and in storm, in the forest or on the sea, it points faithfully and dependably to the north and insures a correct knowledge of true direction. The unmagnetized needle just lies wherever you place it. The magnetizing force which victoriously guides the soul through all the storms of life is the Holy Spirit."

The magnetized needle, which is free to move, cannot help but point to the north constantly. A Spirit-filled Christian cannot help but always be devoted to Christ. The natural man plans and works only for himself, here and now, in this world. A true Christian has discovered that the center of the universe is not himself, but Christ. All that he thinks about, and plans, and devotes himself to, is Christ. His whole Christian life is centered on fearless, unswerving, death-defying, personal loyalty to Christ.

Come, Holy Spirit, heavenly Dove,
With all Thy quickening powers,
Come, shed abroad a Savior's love,
And that shall kindle ours.

ISAAC WATTS.

Chapter IV

WHEN LOVE AWAKENS

T HE GREATEST of these is love."

Lacking love, life loses luster. It takes love to live. The secret of real happiness is love — warm, personal, heaven-born love. Without love we would be only a cold, heartless, noisy gong, or a clanging cymbal.

Without love we might help in doing some useful work of charity, or help to build a church, but not the Kingdom of God. Life is not complete unless we know ourselves as the object of God's deep, abiding love, and also as the channel of enduring, self-sacrificing love to others.

One day our Lord told His disciples, "A new commandment I give to you that you love one another as I have loved you." Jesus said that if the disciples expected to get along with one another, and if they were to go out and make disciples for Him, the secret of their success and blessing would be a firm conviction of God's constant love for them, a glowing, increasing love for Him, as well as a genuine heartfelt love for one another and for all mankind.

In the beginning there had not been much love manifested among the disciples. Some imagined themselves better than the others. Occasionally there would be arguments. Such an atmosphere could not be wholesome for the progress of the cause of the loving Christ. The Lord had to do something for them, in order to enable them to live as He would have them live, and also to carry on the work of extending His Kingdom.

If we permit the Lord thoroughly to search our hearts today, we may find a situation very similar to that among the first disciples. As Christians we may imagine that we love one another, but when we let the Lord scrutinize us under the fluoroscope of his pure love, our love looks rather weak and selfish. In fact, we are often brought to our knees with the straightforward confession before God that our Christian love often runs very low. It becomes cold and is tainted with worldly and selfish ambitions. We are often guilty of an attitude of indifference, contempt, and even anger.

There was a time in the life of St. John when his heart and will were moved, not by love, but by temper and desire for revenge. Because the people in the Samaritan village were not willing to grant lodging to Jesus and His disciples, John wanted to call down fire from heaven to destroy them.

John had also once been quite selfish in his ambitions. When the Kingdom was to be established he desired to sit in the place of honor next to Christ. But as John followed Jesus from day to day and from year to year, he began to observe the pure unselfishness of the Lord. He began to see that Christ never was concerned about His own personal interests, but was always trying to help other people. He saw how devoted Christ was to the true and lasting welfare of others, how kind and thoughtful He was.

When John realized that Christ harbored not the least desire for worldly attainments or honors, he began to relinquish his former selfish ambitions. He began to think, and to pray, and to love as Jesus did. In time John became the disciple "whom Jesus loved," and the apostle of love. As an elderly man, John wrote in one of his epistles, "The elder to the elect lady (congregation) and her children, whom I love in the truth." "If God so loved us, we also ought to love one another," and, "we love, because he first loved us."

Thus it was, more or less, with all the disciples. It was not until after Pentecost that the disciples lost their self-love and began to get along with one another. Then it was that they began to catch a vision of God's saving love for lost humanity and of the vital significance of the Kingdom of God. Then they began to pray in earnest that God would help them to love others as God himself loves them.

How Paul Discovered Love

Bitterness and scorn for God's people once saturated the heart and mind of young Paul. Before his conversion he had no love at all for the Christians, yet he considered himself a qualified religious leader. He imagined that he was rendering the Kingdom of God a distinct service. But when, on the Damascus Road, Paul saw Christ face to face, heard His voice, and realized what kind of person Christ really is, his hateful and contemptuous heart melted. His malice and brutality were transformed into brotherly love and admiration for the disciples. He confessed the perversity of his own heart, and, as the years rolled by, learned the perfect lesson of love.

It was Christ's overflowing love for unconverted Paul that transformed his whole attitude to the program of Christianity. The love of God reflected in the face and in the prayer of dying Stephen had great influence on Paul. The warm, patient, forbearing, hope-inspiring love of Christ constrained Paul to forsake his former manner of life and to dedicate himself to the spreading of the gospel and become zealous for the extension of the Kingdom.

It was this same Paul who has given the world the inspired chapter on love in First Corinthians, "If I speak with the tongues of men and of angels," and so forth. Paul's every epistle radiates the love of God. He often addressed his friends as "my beloved." Paul said, "I hold you in my heart." "God knows that I love you." "My heart's desire and prayer to God is that they may be saved."

"But we were gentle among you, like a nurse taking care of her children. So being affectionately desirous of you, we were ready to share with you, not only the gospel of God, but also our own selves, because you had become very dear to us." "For I wrote you out of much affliction and anguish of heart and with many tears . . . to let you know the abundant love that I have for you."

After his conversion Paul testified about "the Son of God who loved me and gave himself for me." He felt that the love of Christ would go with him farther than anything else of which he could think. Even though he might suffer "tribulation, or distress, or persecution, or famine, or nakedness, or peril, or sword," he was convinced that none of these things could separate him from the vital conviction that Christ loved him. Firmly he believed that "in all these things we are more than conquerors through him who loved us."

Paul became assured that "neither death, nor life, nor angels, nor principalities, nor things present, nor things to come, nor powers, nor height, nor depth, nor anything else in all creation will be able to separate us from the love of God in Christ Jesus our Lord." Paul felt that, whatever might come into his life, the love of God would always be his constant, increasing, victorious, experience.

Paul was convinced that the love of God was stronger than his guilt, stronger than his doubt, stronger than any perversity or weakness of his. In the very center of the circle of God's love, with the love of God all around him, he knew that God would protect him from anything and everything that might ever threaten him.

What God has done with John and Paul and a host of other true followers of Christ, He is willing and able to do with any one of us, if we so desire. If we only confess our own inclination to lovelessness, selfishness, and contempt, and express a genuine desire to be filled with, and to manifest, a true Christian love, God is more than willing to fill our lives to overflowing with His own love.

God's Love Is Deep and Wide

So many people mistrust God because they have not permitted the Holy Spirit to open their hearts to experience the love of the Father. "God is love." Everything that God ever does or tries to do, He does because He loves His people. "Everything that God does with His people, or anything which He permits to happen to them, He does the same as we ourselves would do, if we were in His place, were filled with His love and wisdom and goodness, and could see through all things eternally." In the providence of God there are no accidents. Everything is designed to bring His people to a greater realization of His constant, personal, unselfish love.

Divine love we cannot purchase in the stores, or experimentally discover in any laboratory, or manufacture in any shop. Christian love is a gift from God which He gladly gives to those who permit themselves to be guided by the Spirit.

One of the fruits of spiritual living is love. Love will come of itself by the powerful grace of God when a believer faithfully sits at the feet of Christ, learns of Him, follows Him, bears His cross after Him, and carefully searches out through prayer and Bible study what Christ would do each day and hour, if He were in our place.

The power of God is the love of God. It is because of the Father's love that we are "called the children of God." This love of God is not reserved for His favored children alone.

31

Everyone, even the least worthy, is the object of His warm affection. Paul wrote, "But God shows his love for us in that while we were yet sinners Christ died for us." To wayward Israel the prophet Jeremiah wrote, "I have loved you with an everlasting love; therefore I have continued my faithfulness to you."

A pastor once said, "God's love is all-powerful. A person cannot stop God from loving him. Human love is conditional; one person may love another because of the other's attractiveness, or reputation, or wealth. But God's love is unconditional. God loves everyone, for He is not influenced by the appearances or circumstances of His people, but only by their personal need and by the possibility of their future spiritual development."

It is God's nature to love people. Every person in the world should be told that God loves him. Day by day, in the stores, offices, factories, schools, homes, and on the farms, everywhere, God is seeking to convince people that He loves them. Every person should know where he fits into the eternal plan of things, and all that he needs to do is to make a large room in his life for the entrance of God.

The only people who have been able to help us are they who have loved us and whom we have loved in return. The only people we can help are those whom we love and who love us in return. Even though God loves us, He cannot help us unless we respond to His love and love Him.

In order that we may receive help from God we need to confess that in ourselves we do not love God. But if we pray that God will help us to love Him, He will gladly answer such a prayer. Then God will help us and will make our lives a blessing to himself, to ourselves, and to others. To know God is to love Him.

The Vastness of Christ's Love

There is no love on earth so strong and so irresistible as that which has its source in the unselfish life and the humble and helpful love of Christ. Every word of His is spoken in love. Every act of His was an expression of His love. His answers to requests, whether positive or negative, whether immediate or delayed, are always founded in love. His constant intercession in behalf of His people and those who eventually will become His people, springs forth out of a heart of love.

When the rich young man came to Christ to inquire about the way of salvation, it is said that Jesus "looking upon him loved him." As far as His own attitude was concerned, Christ was ready to go the limit in helping the young man if he were only willing.

When Peter had denied his Lord for the third time, Jesus in love looked at His wayward disciple. It was this look of love which brought Peter to deep repentance, and eventually to sturdy faith and loving, courageous testimony for the Lord who had done so much for him. Christ also loved John with a special love. And we recall that He "loved Martha and her sister and Lazarus."

Every person whom Christ met, He loved. Each one had a different personality, but He loved each one as an individual. He enjoyed the pure luxury of loving them regardless of their differences. Christ loved each individual as if He himself were the only one to care for him; and He loved each one as if that person were the only one on earth to be loved.

We marvel at the mystery of Christ's warm, sacrificial love for us all. No one else has ever loved the individual as Christ has loved. No one else has ever understood the inner needs of the individual as Christ has understood them. No one else has ever done so much good for mankind, directly as well as indirectly, as Christ has done.

No words can ever do full justice to the Son of Mary and the Son of God. He it is who has taught us the best we shall ever know. He it is who has given us the best we shall ever possess. He it is who has given us a vision of the present golden opportunity. He it is who has made us Christians, and He it is who will perfect His own good work already begun in us. Everything He does with us arouses and increases our confidence in Him. Far more important than anything we can do for Him is what He has done for us and what He can do for us and share with us in the future.

It is on account of Christ that God deals so bountifully with us as He does. All the good that we ever enjoy we owe, directly or indirectly, to the work of Christ. All that we ever hope to be, in this life or in the life to come, we owe to Christ alone. Christ alone truly loves us. Christ alone can save us. The miraculous and mysterious love of Christ draws us magnetically to submit ourselves willingly to His best and highest intentions for us all.

What more can we expect Christ to do for us than He has already done, to prove to each of us conclusively that He does love us, and has the right to receive the best of our love, our time, and our talents? When we realize that Christ lived and died to help creatures such as we are, we are drawn to Him with bands of love. We may never be able to understand the mystery of Christ's love, but we are convinced of its reality.

Christ's Love Elicits Our Love

Christ asks for our love to himself. He who is the center of Christianity draws men to himself. To generation after generation He pleads, "Come to me." But in many hearts there is something that holds back; there is something that makes a person hesitate in responding to the love of Christ. What can it be but unbelief, doubt, self-will, or disobedience? Christ is the very best of all. Him we should love above everyone else and everything else. All sin must be confessed, including this sin of not loving Christ as He deserves to be loved.

As a person becomes increasingly attached to Christ, he receives grace to love other things less. Love of self, of pleasure, or of the world, can fatally eclipse our love for Christ. The Apostle whom Jesus loved wrote, "If any one loves the world, love for the Father is not in him." For this reason love for all other things will wisely be put in its proper place in order that our love for Christ may brilliantly and supremely shine in all its merited devotion.

From the early days of the church Christ's love has been both the magnetic and the impelling force that has given direction and inspiration to His followers. Each one who makes room for Christ's love will be passionately and increasingly impelled to learn more and more about Him and to serve Him better. Things that would otherwise be impossible become possible when a person is drawn and driven by the love of Christ.

The great difference between the disciples and the Pharisees was manifested in the increasing love by the disciples and the growing hatred and scorn by the Pharisees. In the beginning the disciples revealed almost as much love for themselves as the Pharisees had for themselves. But as the disciples daily followed their Lord they became transformed by His love, so that their love for God and for their fellowmen increased day by day.

By staying away from Christ, except to find fault with Him, the Pharisees locked their own hearts against His fondest desires for their welfare. Their determined and increasing, unfounded contempt for Him culminated in their crucifying the very One whom God intended that they should have loved supremely.

Personal love for Christ depends largely upon our permitting Him to draw us ever closer to himself in order that we may learn to know Him as He really is, and also to know what He really can do for us. The more we know of Christ the more we want to love Him.

If a magnet becomes demagnetized it can be renewed by bringing it into the field of a strong magnet, or holding it close to a whirling, powerful electrical generator. For us the great unfailing Magnet is Christ. He is the loving and love-inducing Generator of spiritual life and Christian faithfulness.

A man stood for a long time in an art gallery silently gazing at a canvas which showed Christ crucified. No longer could he restrain his feelings, and almost to himself he said, "How can anyone help but love Him, our Savior!" Another man, standing close by, overheard the first man's almost silent testimony. Stepping up he placed his hand on his shoulder, and said, "Brother, I, too, love Him." For awhile the two men stood in silent devotion. Soon they were joined by other visitors who stopped and for a few moments remained quietly reverent, and then went on.

This little group in the art gallery may be increased millions of times as Christians everywhere throughout the world, in city and country, at home and abroad, of every description and kind, add their testimony of love for the Carpenter of Nazareth.

William E. Biederwolf once related an incident which happened in the studio of Gustave Doré. As Doré was putting the delicate finishing touches on one of his famous faces of Christ, a lady stepped quietly into his studio and stood for a moment admiring the touch of Doré's genius. After a while he became aware of her presence and with his usual politeness said, "Pardon me, Madam; I did not know you were here."

"Monsieur Doré," the lady replied, "you must love Him very much to be able to paint Him so well."

"Love Him, Madam," said the great painter, "I should think I do love Him. But if I loved Him more, I would paint* Him better."

If we loved Him more, we would serve Him better.

If we want to be filled with a greater experience of the love of Christ, we need only study the miracle of a flower. In the growth of a flower there is so little that we do; so much that God does. Said Schiller, "What the flower does will-lessly, do thou willingly." The flower opens its petals to welcome whatever may come each day, whether it be sunshine, or rain, or fog. Through the roots and the leaves, the flower gathers and assimilates the elements necessary for its life and development. By yielding itself to the laws of nature the flower develops into its own highest created purpose. In like manner, when we permit Christ to express His love for us, and through us to others, He will fulfill His own best purposes in our life.

It is Christ's love that has inspired Christians, century after century, to dedicate their all and their best to the accomplishment of His loving purposes for men and women everywhere. The glow of Christ's love burns with such zeal and constancy that no power on earth can ever extinguish it. The light of His love shines so brightly that all other devotions are dimmed into relative insignificance.

Do We Really Love Christ?

As Christians we want to scrutinize ourselves to determine whether or not all that we think, say, or do, is the fruit of personal love for Christ. We want to be certain whether or not we are genuine followers of the Holy One of Israel. Do we really love Christ? This is the burning question. Do we really love Christ more than we love any one else? Do we really love Christ more than others love Him? Is our life so directed and inspired as to indicate that we are really drawn and driven by the love of Christ?

Or is there, possibly, some other love and devotion that hinders us from giving the very best of our life to Him who gave His best for each one of us? Not until we have found Christ as the one great Source and Object of our affection will we be advancing toward our own highest spiritual possibilities.

Devotion to a denomination, consecration to a congregation, enthusiasm for some institution, or a tender fondness for traditional forms will sooner or later lose their periodic appeal. Only one motive can be relied upon to keep us in the way of Christian living, and that is the love of Christ for each one of us, a love which draws and compels us to love Him in a manner in which we have never loved anybody else before.

Our love for Christ is difficult to arouse, is undependable, and without the faithful use of the Word of God is likely to fritter away into indifference or contempt. But the love of Christ for human souls is friendly and fervent, gentle and gracious, patient and persistent.

As we sit at His feet and learn of Him, as we partake of the Lord's Supper, as we sit before the cross and meditate on the riches of the saving grace of God in Christ, we feel an overwhelming surge of the sense of incriminating unworthiness. Why should we be the objects of such gracious and hope-inspiring love? If there is anything at all that we can do to show our gratitude for such a complete outpouring of His love to us, undeserving as we are, we want to do it

38

in a spirit of complete devotion and joy, and count it indeed a privilege.

There are many people who respect Christ, or who fear Him. They may admire Him, or honor Him. But to love Christ is something far more significant. He who realizes his utter dependence on the saving grace of Christ will acquire and manifest an ever-increasing measure of true love for Him.

After Peter had denied his Lord three times and saw how willing Christ was to forgive him and to continue to use him in His service, then it was that Peter realized how much Christ loved him, and also how much he loved Christ in return. It is no wonder that Peter out of a full heart exclaimed, "Yes, Lord, you know that I love you." Years later Peter wrote to some friends of his, "Without having seen him you love him."

There are some Christians whose love for Christ at one time burned brightly, but who after a while began to love something else, and whose love for Christ ebbed away into neglect and indifference. To such people God would say, "You have abandoned the love you had at first. Remember then from what you have fallen, repent and do the work you did at first."

Only through repentance, trust and obedience can divine love in human hearts be rekindled. Those who return to Christ will learn to love Him beyond their fondest expectations.

One of our pastors once said, "Christ looked at me and I looked at Him, and we became one forever."

> *I love Thee, because Thou hast first loved me,*
> *And purchased my pardon on Calvary's tree;*
> *I love Thee for wearing the thorns on Thy brow;*
> *If ever I loved Thee, my Jesus, 'tis now.*
>
> *Anonymous.*

Chapter V

SURELY GOODNESS AND MERCY

"WE ARE haunted by an ideal life," declared Phillips Brooks, "and it is because we have within us the beginning and the possibility of such a life." Even though no ordinary person has ever lived the ideal life, it is a fact that God has taken some very ordinary people and by His grace transformed and helped them to perform quite extraordinary accomplishments.

Like Martha of old, many today are troubled and anxious, hurriedly trying to attain a goodness which shall attract attention and trying to win the favor of Almighty God. What will not some people do to try to please the Master and to gain His favor! How people will strain to the limit to get the respect and approval of their friends and acquaintances!

Little do men dream that such efforts really bring no deep or lasting peace with God, or with others, or even with themselves. To this very day people are trying to build their towers to heaven. But what is the result? Only confusion! If people would but open their eyes and behold Jacob's ladder, Christ himself, who already reaches from heaven to earth and who completely satisfies man's deepest needs!

How much better it would be for each of us if we, like Mary, would sit at the feet of Christ and contemplate the things which really belong to righteousness! Whatever goodness there may be is not of human origin but stems from the goodness of God. God would have us simply to look to

Christ and be clothed in His robe of righteousness. Christ wants to transform His people, to help them to do the things that really count, the things that will last forever.

How Man Falls Short of the Glory of God

Those who think the deepest, confess an increasing and painful lack of personal goodness. What we want to do we are not able; and what we want to avoid, that we do. One of the controversies between the Lord and the Pharisees concerned the question of righteousness. Jesus tried to indicate that by His own efforts man can never attain the righteousness which will satisfy the standards of God. The Pharisees falsely and proudly imagined themselves possessing a righteousness which elevated them above the common people.

In the beginning of their discipleship, Peter and some of the others considered themselves quite good men. They were not as bad, at least, as some they knew. But as they continued to follow their Lord they discovered that He had a heart, an attitude, and an accomplishment far superior to their own. After the resurrection they caught a vision of the significance of the higher righteousness of Christ. Then they saw their own shortcomings, became dissatisfied with themselves, and began to hunger for the righteousness and goodness revealed in Christ.

It is not until a person catches a vision of the glory of God's holiness that he can see his own need of anything better than his own goodness. It is only as we make a thorough study of the life of Christ and compare, or rather contrast, ourselves with Him that we begin to appreciate Him. He was without sin! By contrast, how sinful we are! We ought to be thankful for the consciousness of sin, for it makes us appreciate how much we owe to Christ as the Savior from sin.

41

One time after Jesus had been preaching from Peter's boat, He requested Peter to "put out into the deep and let down your nets for a catch." After a moment Peter complied, and the nets enclosed such a great multitude of fishes that the boat began to sink, and they had to call for the other boat. When Peter realized the generosity of Jesus and saw that a miracle had taken place, "he fell down at Jesus' knees, saying, 'Depart from me, for I am a sinful man, O Lord.' " In the presence of the holy and bountiful Savior, Peter keenly felt his own shortcomings.

At first James and John, feeling themselves spiritually qualified, expressed a desire for special places of honor in Jesus' forthcoming cabinet. But as time went on they became impressed by the superior goodness of Christ. In the light of the excellence of Christ they felt the reality of their own imperfections and limitations. In reference to the deep things of faith, they learned to be honest with their own souls and to be honest with God. As the morning fog is dissipated by the rising sun, so the flattery of their friends and their own conceit were soon dissipated by the enlightening rays beaming from the genuine and supreme goodness of the Sun of Righteousness.

There was a time in the life of Paul when he imagined that he was rendering distinguished service to God. He took upon himself the task of uprooting what he considered the pernicious "way" of the Christians. But after he was converted he learned that all his best planning and good work had been only one great offense against the loving Christ. Even as a Christian, when he compared his own thorough schooling in Tarsus and in Jerusalem with the simple unschooled knowledge of the fishermen-disciples, Paul felt that he had a right to call himself an apostle, on an equal footing with the others.

Later, as Paul became better acquainted with the Lord

42

and also with his own heart, he was content to call himself the least of the apostles. He also admitted, since he had persecuted the church of Christ, that he was not worthy to be called an apostle. He was satisfied to be numbered with the saints. Once he said, "I am the very least of all the saints." For a time he was content to be considered a brother among "brothers."

Toward the end of his busy life, after he had thoroughly meditated upon what he had seen when he was caught up into the heavens and saw things unspeakably holy, he was willing to testify that he was saved by the grace of Christ who had come into the world "to save sinners. And I am the foremost of sinners." It was because Paul had come very close to the supreme holiness and the brilliant goodness of the Lord that he discovered himself increasingly to be the chief of sinners.

When Job was prosperous and well he considered himself a reasonably good man. But when he lost everything, even his health, he turned to God, and God revealed himself to Job. When Job saw the eternal majesty and rapturous glory of the Lord, he confessed, "I despise myself, and repent in dust and ashes." After such a confession on the part of Job, God was pleased to restore to him his health and other blessings.

When King Uzziah died, Isaiah felt he had lost his very best friend. He felt that now the government would be jeopardized; never again could they get such a good king. For comfort, reflection and rest, Isaiah went into the temple. There the Lord, the King and Friend who could not die, revealed himself to Isaiah. He saw the Lord, high and lifted up, in all His beauty of holiness. In the bright light of God's majesty and supreme righteousness Isaiah caught a vision of his own unholiness and unrighteousness.

"Woe is me!" Isaiah cried out, "for I am lost; for I am a

43

man of unclean lips." As soon as Isaiah had made his confession, the Lord sent His angel with a coal of fire from the altar. Isaiah's guilt was forgiven; he was cleansed, and was made a child of God. And then God sent him out on an errand that had spiritual significance.

Said Bishop Andrewes, "Woe is me! That I did not reverence nor dread the incomprehensibleness of Thy glory, Thy tremendous power, the awfulness of Thy presence, Thy strict justice, Thy lovable goodness."

We who are more or less geared into the organization of some church, or charity, or useful activity, sometimes find ourselves confronted by the realization of the presence, the holiness, and the love of a personal God. Then it is, also, that we discover the naked truth about our own inadequacy. At times there seem to come inspiring moments of great spiritual exaltation, but at other times there steal upon us periods of inky smog of temptation, doubt, and even sin, when the glory of the Lord seems completely hidden. One of our Bible teachers used to say, "A Christian is one who is so bad a sinner that he needs Jesus Christ as his Savior." What counts most before God is not our sin, but the blood of Jesus which cleanses us from all sin.

Because we want to become better Christians, shall we therefore excuse our weaknesses? Shall we imagine, for instance, that because we want to be moral people, or attend some church, or are interested in some community uplift, we may be excused if we do not always live up to our own highest ideals? Or is sin in the life of the Christian just as hateful to God as the sins of other people?

It is safe to say that the sins of Christians are more offensive than the sins of other people. Other people may not know better, but Christians know, or ought to know, what is right. There is hardly anything that causes such hindrance to the cause of Christ as the backslidings of those

44

who profess to be followers of Christ. The sins of Christians are not by nature more serious, but their seriousness is increased by the worthiness of the Christ, to whom they have committed themselves.

In 396 A.D. when the wild hordes of invaders burst into the Roman Empire, Hieronymus wrote to a friend, "It is because of our own sinfulness that the barbarians are strong. Because of our vices the Roman Empire will fall. We are unfortunate in having so displeased God that His wrath turns against us through the raging of these vandals."

Augustine observed that it was the unlearned and simple-minded people who stood up and accepted the Kingdom of God for themselves, while the learned and "good" people were content to grovel in their sinfulness, pride, and indifference.

Sin is no mere delusion. It is a falling short of the glory of God. "Anything that is contrary to the will of God is sin." "Anything that separates us from God or from other people is sin." "Any deviation from the standard of perfection revealed in and by Jesus Christ is sin." "Whatever does not proceed from faith is sin." "Whoever knows what is right and fails to do it, for him it is sin." As J. B. Phillips says, "It is the straight-edge of the Law that shows us how crooked we are."

We never really perceive the power of our sinfulness until we try to get rid of it. As we meditate upon the genuine holiness of God in His Word, and as we realize the perversity of our own hearts, we become more willing to confess our utter dependency upon the satisfying mercy of God. We can never reform ourselves or others. Others cannot transform us. It is only as we become willing to be led to the feet of Christ that He can transform us and give us a newness of life. It has been said, "Though we are stubborn in our sin, God is more stubborn in showing His mercy."

Jesus once told a parable about the invitations to a wedding. There is a tradition that, according to Oriental custom, when the host extended an invitation to his friends for a wedding he also provided each guest with a special robe. All the guests would then be on an equal footing, and would honor their host by wearing the wedding garment.

But one man scorned the wedding garment; he came dressed in his own clothing. In his independence and arrogance he wanted to be different from the rest. The host would have none of it. He ordered his servants: "Bind him hand and foot, and cast him into the outer darkness."

No one can ever stand acquitted before the judgment throne of the righteous God because of his prayers or kindnesses or any other good works. "By works of the law shall no one be justified." "God is the enemy of our best, for our best is only filthy rags in His sight."

A teacher in one of our Bible schools once said, "If we add one iota to the righteousness of Christ, it will not be the righteousness of Christ. Christ's righteousness becomes ours when we believe in Him and accept Him as our Savior.

GOD REVEALS A RIGHTEOUSNESS BY GRACE

Although no one may enter before the presence of God in his own "garb" there is a "wedding garment" offered to anyone who will wear it. This wedding garment is the righteousness of Christ. We do not deserve to wear this wedding garment, but anyone who accepts Christ as personal Savior puts on this special garment; he "puts on" Christ himself. For "Christ is our righteousness." God made Jesus Christ "our wisdom, our righteousness and sanctification and redemption."

When a person confesses his own utter lack of the goodness and righteousness which God requires, he begins to

46

manifest the kind of spirit that God likes to see. The only fitness that God requires is to feel our need of Him. "God's kindness is meant to lead you to repentance," and faith. When a person permits God to give him true repentance, he also opens his heart and life to an increasing experience of the overwhelming goodness of God. Confession gives working room for God.

If we should find ourselves eternally condemned in lowest hell, we should have to admit that God is just in sending us there because of our sinfulness. But God is more than just. God is also merciful. With Him there is forgiveness. Time and again He has had mercy upon us. And he who trusts in this abounding mercy of God will discover the assurance of full salvation for which he has been hungering.

The experience of a believer is somewhat similar to that of Abraham. Abraham and Sarah were childless. For years they had wanted a child. One day the message came from God that in due time a son would be born to them. "Abraham believed God, and it was reckoned to him as righteousness." In his own life Abraham was not any more righteous than others, but he trusted that God is righteous in keeping His promises. And God counted, or imputed, or reckoned, Abraham's faith for righteousness.

The kind of righteousness which God found in Abraham was the righteousness of believing that the promises of God are true, and trustworthy, and in due time will be fulfilled. Abraham manifested a humble reverence, willingly permitting the wise and benevolent goodness of God to operate in his heart and life.

When the penitent publican in the temple cried out, "God, be merciful to me a sinner," Jesus said of him, "This man went down to his house justified," that is, the man was counted righteous; he was saved. In the same manner God stands ready to save anyone at all who pleads for mercy,

47

confessing that he has no righteousness of his own, and trusting "him who justifies the ungodly." His faith is counted for righteousness.

He who looks in faith to Christ on the cross is counted as though he (the believer) died on the cross for his own sin. From that moment of penitence and faith, God counts the believer as His own child. Henceforth God looks at him through Christ, and bestows upon him a share in the righteousness of Christ.

When the prodigal son fully realized the attractive and compelling love of his Father and thus "came to himself," he straightway returned home. The happy father ordered his servants, "Bring quickly the best robe, and put it on him; and put a ring on his hand, and shoes on his feet; and bring the fatted calf and kill it, and let us eat and make merry; for this my son was dead, and is alive again; he was lost, and is found."

At that moment, as always, the Father treated his son as though he had always been his son, and as though he had never sinned at all. For when God forgives, he also forgets, thinking only of the present, joyous relationship. In like manner God stands ready to reveal to us His constant goodness and mercy. Thus God begins and continues the conquest of sin by offering us His complete forgiveness and joy. Said Isaiah, "Though your sins are like scarlet, they shall be as white as snow; though they are red like crimson, they shall become like wool."

Jesus stepped into our place and accepted what we deserve in order that we may step into His place and receive what He deserves. He accepted our sin as His own in order that He may share with us His own righteousness and goodness.

It is only as we deal with the deepest needs of our hearts and lives that we can ever become real children of God. We are worthy of participating in the Kingdom of God only as we are keenly aware of our own absolute unworthiness. It is only by the grace of God that we may enter a church, or open a Bible, or live in His Kingdom.

What a marvel it is that God can take a human being, just as he is, wash him clean in the blood of the Lamb, give him a right spirit of penitence and trusting faith, and make him a blessing for all humanity!

As long as the disciples considered themselves good and in need of nothing, they were of little or no use to the Master. As long as their hearts were filled with their own righteousness, there was no room for the righteousness of Christ. Not until the Lord permitted their self-righteousness to find expression in various acts of irresponsibility and perversity were they emptied of their self-importance and began to seek the higher righteousness revealed in Christ.

Too often we trust in our own goodness rather than in the goodness of God. A pastor said, "What counts is not what we do, but what God is." The human race suffers from the deception of imagining that it is better than it really is. In the constant presence of God a person can boast of no righteousness of his own.

A little righteousness is a dangerous thing, for it is likely to make a person self-satisfied, instead of arousing in him a desire to get closer to God. We must never be content to dwell on the prairies of human goodness when the mountain peaks of God's higher righteousness beckon us ever upward and onward.

If our faith were but more simple,
We should take Him at His Word;
And our lives would be all sunshine
In the presence of our Lord.

FREDERICK WILLIAM FABER.

49

Chapter VI

TRUSTING THE GRACE OF GOD

WHEN John Wesley was on a ship on the Atlantic headed for the state of Georgia in the United States, he met some Moravian missionaries who influenced him deeply. In a storm when all the other passengers were frightened the Moravians were perfectly calm. "We have given our lives to God," they said. "We are in God's hands. We have nothing to fear."

Wesley was unable to share their assurance of being children of God. For several years he had been seeking for peace in his soul. In all his missionary activities or in personal endeavors he could not find any satisfactory experience of the assurance of salvation.

After returning to England Wesley was invited to a meeting of the Moravian Society in London. He did not want to go, for he felt that in some respects he was as good a man as they, maybe even better. Yet he was convinced that they possessed something vital that was sorely lacking in his own life.

"I went very unwillingly," said Wesley, "to a Moravian Society in Aldersgate, where a layman was reading Luther's 'Introduction to the Epistle to the Romans.'" These are some of the words: "Faith is God's work in us which changes us and gives us a new life from God. This faith is a living, busy, active, powerful thing. Such a faith makes us joyful, bold, and full of warm love toward God and all created things."

"About a quarter of nine," Wesley continued, "while listening to Luther's description of the change which the Spirit works in the heart through faith in Christ, I felt my heart strangely warmed. I felt I did trust in Christ, Christ alone for salvation, and an assurance was given me that He had taken away my sins, even mine, and saved me from the law of sin and death. I am happy in Him. I am saved by His grace."

Luther once said that if anybody in the world could have been saved by his own righteousness and good works, it was he. Luther did everything humanly possible to become a good man, but found it increasingly and distressingly impossible. Then one day he discovered the saving truth, "He who through faith is righteous shall live," and, "God justifies him who has faith in Jesus."

Luther made diligent study and learned further that a person is "justified by faith in Christ and not by the works of the law." "Through him (Christ) we have obtained access to this grace in which we stand," and "While we were yet sinners Christ died for us." When Luther became willing to believe this, he was satisfied to be saved, not according to his own plan, but according to God's plan of salvation. Then he said, "The cross of Christ is our only hope."

Years later John Bunyan said, "I was broken to pieces by the holiness of God. I squirmed and was exceedingly restless under the burden of guilt that was upon me." Bunyan then studied Luther's *Commentary on the Epistle to the Galatians,* and there discovered "this grace wherein we stand."

Said Bunyan, "Luther led me out of man's good opinion of his own righteousness and his willingness to justify himself in his own eyes by merit of his own performance, to Christ as the giver of abundant grace to the chief of sinners."

For a long time people imagined that the earth was the

center of the solar system and of the universe, in other words, that the sun and all the stars moved around the earth. But science now teaches us that the center of the solar system is not the earth, but the sun.

In like manner a large number of people imagine that they themselves are the center of interest, and that everybody else and everything else was created to serve them alone. But when people become better acquainted with all creation they realize that the center of the universe is God Himself.

A believer depends for salvation and sanctification, not on himself, but on Christ. A believer has faith, not in his own goodness, but in the goodness of God. The essence of real living finds its purpose and climax in being grateful that Christ lived not for Himself, but for others, including us, and also that our lives develop to their utmost by living, not for ourselves, but for others.

All shortcomings are manifestations of uncontrolled, strong, personal desire, aggravated by a feeling of fear or inferiority, or by striving to gain personal recognition. A person's life would become greatly enriched if he could get his mind off himself so that the center of his life could be concentrated on God. Then he could dedicate himself so that God could use him as a channel of blessing to others.

ALL THE DAYS OF MY LIFE

The faith that saves a person also begins to change his life. When a person is saved by faith and gives his love to God, the Holy Spirit's work of purification continues in earnest. God sent His Son into the world to save people, not in sin, but from sin. Making people holy, as well as saving them, is God's work.

When a person comes ever closer to God, he begins to learn how much God in His rich grace has already done for him. He realizes what kind of creature he would have been without God. He sees how much more remains for God to do in his life. He begins to hunger and to thirst after more complete righteousness than he has ever experienced before.

God wants, not only to save a person, but also to make him holy and meet for His use. In this life a Christian can never become satisfied with himself. God has not yet completed His work of cleansing us. We are not yet wholly sanctified. We are not yet completely created. We are only being made. We are not a being, but a becoming. This life is not health, but recovery; not rest, but labor. But we can safely trust ourselves into the hands of Christ who is able to perfect the good work which He himself has begun in us.

As long as a person lives, there is always more to which to look forward. An ideal overtaken is no longer an ideal. The Pharisees were satisfied with their meager attainments; they had nothing more to learn. But the closer a person comes to Christ, the farther his ideal seems to advance before him.

Like the advancing pillar of fire, the yearning for perfection becomes an ingrained desire which can never be completely satisfied in this life. "Ideals are like stars," Carl Schurz used to say, "we never reach them, but like mariners at sea, we chart our course by them."

Every Christian is a revelation of what he has permitted Christ to do in his life. The life of a Christian is a living demonstration of what God can do for people. When a person knows the possible waywardness of his own life, he yearns for, seeks, and clings to a safe Guide.

One day in the Orient a tourist visited the shop of a silversmith. The tourist became interested in watching a crucible of molten silver over an intensely hot flame. With skilled hand, an apprentice, with a small ladle, was removing the scum as it kept rising to the surface and throwing it to one side.

"How long do you need to keep the silver on the fire?" inquired the tourist. "How do you know when the silver is properly refined and ready for use?" "The silver will be ready," replied the apprentice, "when the master comes and can see in the surface of the silver the clear and perfect image of his own face."

What we call trials are really God's fires to cleanse and purify us from that which is wasteful and harmful in our lives. God will not permit the fires to destroy us. He intends only to consume the dross and to refine and purify the real gold and silver of Christian trust and faith.

God wants to help the believer to devote his life and energy to the things worth while, the things that have spiritual significance. In the Providence of God, Christ will continue His work of cleansing in us and in due time by grace see in the Spirit-cleansed lives of His redeemed people the clear reflection of His own face.

When a person trusts in the goodness of God for salvation, God gives him grace to deal with other people according to the Golden Rule. A true believer wants his life to be "worthy of the gospel of Christ." His behavior in all things becomes a safe example for others to follow. As his eyes become opened to the work of the Lord, he begins to realize the vast amount of good which the Lord is doing every day in and through the lives of His consecrated people.

When temptation comes, he accepts it as an opportunity to choose what is right. At all times the goodness and the mercy of God is his inspiration and ideal.

Many will agree with the testimony of a business man in Minneapolis, Minnesota, who once said, "The longer I live the more I realize how satisfying is the all-sufficient grace of God."

54

Chapter VII

PEACE, BE STILL

H E LEADS me beside the still waters."
   "How can the muddy water become clear?" inquired Lao-tze, the Chinese philosopher. "Let it be still,
and it will gradually become clear." When a person can
bring himself to an attitude of quietness and make himself
remain still, many of the problems of life will settle and
solve themselves.

All worth-while accomplishments have been labored upon
in secret. A business man often makes his most important
decisions in the dead of night when he is all alone. The most
important decisions in a court trial are usually studied out
beforehand behind closed doors. Emerson observed that the
"things of a man for which we visit him were done in the
dark and the cold."

Worthy accomplishments in science, literature, art, religion, manufacturing, selling, advertising, building construction, and so forth, find their real foundation in many
hours and years of quiet study and planning. Napoleon sat
for hours at a time in deep thought before he proceeded to
issue an important command. Washington spent much time
in prayer and meditation, for he realized that important results for his whole country for all time to come depended
upon wise decisions.

Always it pays to take time for rest, reflection, and meditation. John Ruskin said wisely, "The rests are as much a
part of the music as the notes, and we contribute just as

much to the music by observing the rests as by playing the notes."

The Blessing of Being Quiet

In the numerous activities of life we study all kinds of projects, but it would be well if we could also "study to be quiet." If the human heart is to be filled with the best blessings of heaven, we must be still and learn that it is not we who are God, but God is God.

He who desires to be a channel of blessing from God to man must hold himself quiet in order to receive the blessings which God wants to share with him. God reveals His glory and majesty, not in the storm or in the earthquake, but in the gentlest whisper which is heard only when we are perfectly quiet.

A Quaker went one day to visit Klaus Harms in Kiel, Germany. Harms confessed that he was so busy and had so much to do that he hardly had time to speak with visitors. "Since you have so much to do," inquired the Quaker, "and you have to speak so often, how can you find time to be quiet to listen to what the Spirit has to say to you?"

The Quaker's words struck Harms with great spiritual force. Harms began to take more time for Bible reading and meditation. Becoming strengthened in his inner life he began to conserve his scattered energies and to accomplish a work of higher quality.

It takes time to find peace with God, with oneself, and with one's fellow men. It takes time to think out things deeply, intensely, completely, and relatedly. It takes time and labor to search out and to find rest and solid foundation on the spiritual bedrock for one's soul and life; but it pays immensely in every way.

Time is well spent when a driver stops his automobile at a gasoline station in order that fuel, oil, water, and air may be replenished. Time is not wasted when a person sits down to enjoy his regular meals. Time is well invested when a person stops to sharpen a dull tool, to wash a mirror, to clean house, or to study a road map. It pays immeasurably when a person takes time to read his Bible, to let God replenish, feed, sharpen, cleanse, and re-direct his spiritual purposes in life.

As Walter S. Landor said, "Quietness is the reception room to God; only one more step, and you can stand in His immediate presence."

Goethe has wisely said, "No one can produce anything of value unless he isolates himself."

The founder of the China Inland Mission, J. Hudson Taylor, affirmed, "Christ is always ready for communion with a prepared heart."

Occasionally in the desert one finds a few trees. Some are stunted. A person marvels that it is possible for any trees at all to grow in the desert. But if one should take a shovel and try to trace the roots, he would find the roots growing deep and far in search of precious moisture. In like manner, in a troublous world, a person who takes time to thrust his spiritual roots deep and far into the Word and the peace of God will be spiritually invigorated and strengthened in his soul. God will enable such a person to endure many more trials than those who neglect these enriching privileges.

Peace of soul and mind and heart is a gift from God. Truly it is a golden treasury of heavenly tranquillity. He who makes room for the peace of God experiences the soul's sweet contentment in God. More than all else that God can give us, we need most just to rest in God Himself. When a person turns to God in genuine repentance and trusting faith, God will gladly flood his soul with the assurance of His grace and peace.

In each of Paul's letters his salutation always included the phrase, "Grace and peace." "Grace to you, and peace, from God our Father, and the Lord Jesus Christ"; "Grace be unto you, and peace"; "Grace, mercy, and peace."

Paul knew from experience that when he discovered the saving grace of God he also found peace as the fruit of that grace. It is never peace first, and then grace; but always grace first, and then peace. Blessed is he who, in our day, can rest his soul and his life in the all-sufficient grace of God. Then immediately follow peace with God, peace with oneself, and peace in one's attitude toward one's fellow men. "Therefore, since we are justified by faith, we have peace with God through our Lord Jesus Christ."

The great trouble maker in human life is sin. Greed, envy, jealousy, selfish ambition, anger, disobedience to God, stubbornness and pride are persistent disturbers of man's peace of soul. The real solution for finding peace of heart is to become willing, through Bible study and prayer, to let God have His way in our lives.

When we become willing to walk with God in all obedience, humility, and contentment, God quickly raises the shades of our chaotic souls and enables the sunlight of His joyful and restful peace to make us glad all the days of our lives. Many are the souls who have experienced the truth of St. Augustine's words: "Thou hast made us for Thyself; and our hearts are restless until we find rest in Thee."

CHRIST TOOK TIME TO BE QUIET

For seeking and discovering peace of soul, man's most inspiring example is always Christ. Every day and night, the Lord took time to spend some moments or hours with His heavenly Father in prayer and intercession.

John R. Mott observed, "If the hill back of Nazareth could

give forth its secret, if the Sea of Galilee could tell what it witnessed, if the desert places round about Jerusalem could tell their story, if the Mount of Olives could speak out and tell us what transpired there, they would tell us, more than anything else, of the prayer life of the Lord. They would reveal its intensity, its unselfishness, its constancy, its godly fear that made it irresistible."

It was Jesus' habit of taking time for unhurried prayer and meditation that enabled Him to meet the problems and trials of life with peace and composure. Because He lived close to the heart of God He was not aggravated by the common disturbances of everyday life. As deep breathing is refreshing for the body, so Christ knew that real prayer is refreshing to the soul.

As a person looks up to the mighty mountains he realizes something of their great mass and permanency. So to Christ the study of the Scriptures was a looking up to the unfathomable majesty and power of God. Storms come and go but the mountains remain. When a person studies the blueprints of a great building he can understand something of what is being constructed. When a person studies the Bible he learns something of God's great plan for the universe.

The source of our peace of heart is Christ himself. Christ "is our peace." He is the peacemaker of the heart. His first coming was intended to bestow "peace on earth." In the storms of doubt, guilt, and despair He still speaks His "Peace, be still." Even today, to trusting souls, there comes a great calm. When Christ is permitted to have His way in the homes, businesses, and lives of His people, we can rest and work in assured peace.

To all who need Him, Christ extends His gracious invitation, "Come to me, all who labor and are heavy-laden, and I will give you rest. Take my yoke upon you, and learn from me; for I am gentle and lowly in heart, and you will find rest for your souls. For my yoke is easy, and my burden is light."

Christ's coming was intended to reconcile man with God, and to proclaim to harassed humanity the promise of God's peace. When Christ died on the cross, He satisfied God's requirements for justice and righteousness. At Calvary the sin of the world was atoned; the greatest thing that ever happened, happened at Calvary.

When Christ died, He redeemed all mankind to God, past, present, and future. But only those people receive the full benefit of His redemptive work and find peace with God who are willing to let the Lord open their hearts for the entrance of Christ, and permit Him to produce in their hearts repentance, trusting faith, ready obedience, and sincere gratitude. Then comes peace, real peace, God's peace.

When the Lord was ready to lay down His life for the disciples He said, "Peace I leave with you; my peace I give to you." He wanted His disciples to enjoy His peace as a lifetime gift. Although we may at times forget about it, the peace of Christ remains constantly effective. When we look in faith to the redemptive work of Christ we have His peace; we own it; we cherish it.

Paul said, "Let your requests be made known to God. And the peace of God, which passes all understanding, will keep your hearts and your minds in Christ Jesus." It is not we who are to keep the peace of Christ. Too often we forget about it. Rather, it is the peace of God that keeps us—our hearts and our minds. It sustains us, supports us, encourages us, protects us.

Communion with God Gives Us Real Peace

Dwight L. Moody once said, "The most precious moments I have had with God were not experienced before large congregations, but when I sat alone at the feet of Jesus. In our modern times we do not take time to listen to what Jesus has to tell us. We are so busy that we do not choose the good part. If we did what was right, we would spend more time in listening, and when we did speak, it would be only when we had something worth while to say."

When Jenny Lind was at the very height of her popularity as a concert singer, she retired to a simple home in the country. The remainder of her life she wanted to spend in quietness and peace. Since people were eager to pay thousands to hear her sing, her numerous friends could not understand her strange action. A reporter went to inquire from her the reason for her leaving the concert stage.

After the usual courteous greetings, the reporter asked Jenny Lind why she had discontinued her concerts. She smiled ever so sweetly, pointed to the sunset and to a Bible in her lap, and replied. "You do not understand. The world was very kind, but it was making me forget the sunset, and it made me forget my Bible. What else could I do?" In the Word of God and in communion with nature she came closer to the central joys and deep satisfactions of life than in the clamorous applause of thousands of her admirers.

When John R. Mott would arrive at his office for his daily work, the first half hour of the day was spent behind closed doors in reading and meditating on some Bible passage, and in prayer. Mott's associates respected his determined desire to be alone for a time, and he received no calls or visitors during those precious minutes. He found that these moments of meditation gave him safe direction, composure, inspiration, and divine fellowship for the day.

In one of his stories, "Buried Alive," Arnold Bennett tells of a woman who became tired and wearied with the increasing whirl of parties and social functions. Annoyed and bored to utter bewilderment and confusion she was good company neither for others nor for herself.

After some months she began reading the Bible. Her friends were amazed that she was neglecting her social life and thought she was becoming strange. One day she came upon the words, "Be still, and know that I am God." She did not understand the words, but they seemed to hold promise of something that she needed. But how could she make herself still? There was too much to do; too many places to go.

The lady quoted the verse to some of her friends, but they did not seem to know what she was talking about. After many days and much meditation, it dawned on her that only God could make her still. Only God could make her realize that long before she was born, God was God, and many trusting souls had found peace in God. After she was dead, God would still be God. And so it happened that this Bible verse became to this lady a voice from another world. We do not find peace in other people or even in ourselves. Our peace is centered in God himself.

A single verse from Scripture contains spiritual effectiveness and power and peace for anyone who will thoroughly meditate on it and get from its core the peace and blessing which God wants to share with the diligent seeker. It is only in constant communion with God in His holy Word that a person can establish, preserve and deepen his peace of heart and mind.

In many lands the Bible is a best seller. And yet we sin woefully against ourselves, against God, and against others in failing to take more time to read it unhurriedly. God is waiting to meet us in His Word. If we listen carefully, God will speak with us. How can God speak peace to our hearts unless we take time to listen thoughtfully to His still, small voice!

Sometimes it is beneficial to read a whole Bible book at a time, like Ruth, or Esther, or Galatians, or Ephesians. It takes only fifteen or twenty minutes to read through some of the shorter of Paul's epistles. It takes only a minute to read through some of the Psalms of David. (Some people read through the Psalms of David at least once a year.) It takes only thirty seconds to pray the Lord's prayer, only fifteen seconds to lift the heart to God in the doxology. Sometimes all that a person needs is part of a chapter, or a single Bible verse, or even a portion of a verse, to send him off spiritually fortified for the day.

We *have* time for God each day; all we need to do is to take time for God.

News is important. A Christian cannot help but be interested in what happens to people all about him. But it is infinitely more important to learn what happens to people spiritually, or what can help them spiritually. Most of what really matters to people never gets into the newspapers.

Many have come to feel that it is more important to read what Jesus has to say to our generation than what some reporter or columnist has to tell us. Surely it is just as important to know what Isaiah, or Paul, or Peter has to say as to read the latest news.

Many people read a portion of Scripture the first thing in the morning. Not the morning newspaper, not the radio or television, not a magazine, or a secular book, but the Bible. After the Bible reading, one can read other material, or listen to people, with a sort of divine perspective.

In the Bible we discover God's peaceful purposes toward mankind: "For I know the plans I have for you . . . . plans for welfare." Turning to God, Isaiah said, "Thou dost keep him in perfect peace, whose mind is stayed on thee." Turning to the people Isaiah said, "In quietness and in trust shall be your strength." In retiring at night King David, com-

63

mending himself into the hands of God, could say, "In peace I will both lie down and sleep; for thou alone, O Lord, makest me dwell in safety."

Faith Follows the Leadership of God

Peace of soul is appreciably promoted and strengthened when a person becomes willing to accept all things as from the hand of God. Because of what his Savior and Lord has done for him, he is willing to endure anything at all, if only it will glorify God. He knows that his life is in the hands of God. He accepts everything as an opportunity of receiving some new blessing from God.

Much of what we call restlessness or trouble is nothing but unwillingness on our part to do what we clearly know God wants us to be doing. "Faith is not strain; it is repose." Like Christ in Gethsemane, a person comes to know that God has greater plans for us than we have. When a person prays, "I do not care what happens to me, only that Thy will may be done in and through me," he will discover the peace that passes all understanding.

On earth there is found no absolute, permanent peace of mind. At best it can only be comparative, or relative. But even this proves to be indescribably refreshing. Two artists endeavored to paint a picture entitled, "Peace." One sketched a landscape in which not so much as a breath of air disturbed the foliage of the trees or ruffled the placid water of a pool. The quietness of death reigned.

But the other artist caught a more practical vision of peace. A wind-swept tree grew perilously close to the brink of a tumultuous waterfall. Suspended from a swaying branch hung a nest on which the mother bird was sitting confidently at rest, perfectly calm and peaceful in spite of the raging current that seemed to leap at the tiny home in a vain attempt to wash it down to destruction. In spite of various dangers, in the tranquil breast of the bird there dwelt only the spirit of calm, composure, and contentment.

Is it not true that often we plan to do some work, or to go some place, but something intervenes to frustrate our best laid plans? But who knows but that what we call disturbances, or frustrations, or interferences, or hindrances, may be God's guidance eventually to bring us a much richer blessing than if we had been permitted to do what we had wanted to do?

When American troops entered a certain city in Italy, which had been heavily bombed, they discovered the philosopher Santayana calmly reading a book. Someone asked him, "How can you sit and read a book in this terrible bombardment?" Santayana calmly replied, "I am a philosopher, and philosophy is a long study. I have trained my mind to dwell on eternal matters."

Our Lord does not take us out of the trials and dangers of life. Instead, God goes with His people into the midst of their fiery furnaces, into the midst of their storms, there to strengthen, purify, and encourage them, giving them ever richer experiences of His all-sufficient grace which they could never have had in any other way. When a person is determined to obey God at all costs, he discovers the presence, the peace, and the power of God as never before.

Even in the midst of most difficult problems our hearts can find rest in God. "My presence will go with you, and I will give you rest." In such an assurance comes peace, serene, sustaining, satisfying.

> *The soul that on Jesus hath leaned for repose,*
> *I will not, I cannot desert to His foes:*
> *That soul, though all hell should endeavor to shake,*
> *I'll never—no, never, no, never forsake.*
>
> "K" in Rippon's Selection, 1787.

Chapter VIII

PEACE WITH MY FELLOW MEN

BEFORE a good orchestra or band begins its concert all the instruments are tuned to a standard pitch. Usually *a* is played on the tuba, for the tuba has a correct, invariable pitch. If the concert master has a true pitch he may play an *a*. In a small orchestra *a* may be played on the piano. All the other instruments, then, are harmonized with the one instrument that is known to be true to pitch.

When a piano tuner prepares to tune a piano he first strikes a tuning fork, usually the note *a*, and tunes the *a* note (above middle c) on the piano. The tuning fork is used because of its dependable, unvarying pitch. Then the other notes on the piano are corrected to harmonize with the tuned *a*.

One instrument that is off-key can spoil the rendition of a whole orchestra. Musical instruments which are perfectly tuned to the standard pitch will beautifully harmonize with other tuned instruments.

When a person is going to work with other people, what is going to be the basis of harmony and accord? Where shall he find a dependable, unvarying spiritual and moral "pitch," so that all the people in the world may find a basis of agreement and harmony?

Is it selfish ambition? Is it personal display? Is it personal success? Is it possibly the welfare of the public? Is it the moral law? Is it the will of God, the Creator of all? One person who is out of harmony with God may bring disharmony and eventual failure even among a group of Christians. But people who are yielded to obey God at all costs will beautifully harmonize and co-operate with other God-fearing and God-loving persons.

The secret of peace is for each one to get right with God. The love of God is the spiritual tuning-fork which really helps to bring harmony among His people. He who enjoys peace with God wants to have peace with the rest of the world, at least as far as his own attitude is concerned. Since God thinks thoughts of peace toward all the world, a Christian also wants to think thoughts of peace to all his fellow men.

Peace with God yields a sense of peaceableness with one's fellow men. When we know of God's love for all mankind, He will enable us also to love everyone else with His own love. When we learn to love people, it becomes possible, under God, to live in harmony with them. One of the richest fruits of spiritual living is a spirit of good will and harmony with one's fellow-Christians. However long a friendship may exist, one needs to be careful to ward off thoughts, words or deeds that arouse suspicion and misunderstanding. How a person needs to be on guard at all times to maintain understanding and good will!

Hell is hell because of disorder, confusion and self-will. Heaven is heaven because of peace and harmony with God, the Concert Master of the universe. Our life on earth is a prelude to the one or the other, depending upon our own way of life.

Divisions, misunderstandings, and contentions seem to plague some groups and some individuals like a frightful epidemic, or a vast armada of bombers. Some people seem to be most happy when they can spread abroad the word of gossip and suspicion and arouse dissension and quarreling.

They seem to enjoy throwing around them the tear-gas bombs of unkind criticism and fault-finding.

Satan and his servants are pledged to cause all kinds of trouble in order that they may hinder the progress and growth of the Kingdom of God. Satan's determination is to divide and destroy the forces on the side of God. The devil is never so happy as when he can use a professing Christian as an instrument for causing discord.

How Abraham Made Peace

One great cause of disharmony among people is insistence on personal rights. And when others, too, from a different viewpoint demand their personal rights the result is friction and discord. No person has a right to all his rights. A peace minded person is willing to yield some of his own rights for the sake of peace and harmony.

The shepherds and cowboys of Abraham and Lot quarreled about the pasture lands and wells of water. Abraham, being a man of peace, was willing to give up some of his own God-given personal rights to any part of the Promised Land which Lot might select. In his greed Lot chose the best pastureland in the Jordan Valley. But eventually Lot gained little or nothing except trouble for himself and his family. When Sodom and Gomorrah were destroyed he almost lost his own life. Abraham permitted himself to be cheated, but God was with him, and Abraham had plenty, and to spare. Whatever is gained by force must be maintained by force; and eventually will be lost to a still greater force. What is won by peaceful methods is kept longer and enjoys the goodwill of men and the blessing of God.

In almost every group, whether large or small, there is likely to be some individual who wants to be the dictator. He may be unselfish, or he may be selfish. But in the rise to power, even good power, there may be occasional clashes. How few people are really tolerant of the rights and privileges of others! How few are willing to listen to the viewpoints of others! How necessary it is for each individual to guard against the desire to be master of all. Rather, in the spirit of Jesus, be the servant of all!

The sword of Peter has no place in the Kingdom of the Prince of Peace. In His conquest of the world, Christ has no need for an army bent on destruction. Christ came, not to help one man conquer another, but to help each man to conquer himself. Christ's mission on earth was, not by means of force to found a political and military kingdom, but by peace, love, and good will to establish a spiritual kingdom for the welfare of every individual. He came, not to impose heavy burdens, but to give people the richest possible blessings.

Often a man's worst enemy is himself. Within his own heart there lives a spirit which may cause untold harm. Sometimes a person is tempted to do things, and to say things in a spirit of evil temper and rage. But such a spirit had better be put in its proper place, so that a person will be kept from disturbing the peace of his fellow men, and his own peace as well.

The strongest arguments are often clothed in the gentlest words. A peaceable answer turns away wrath and strife. Sometimes peace may be promoted by a word wisely and softly spoken, but often the ways of peace are best encouraged by a person keeping absolutely quiet. When it is storming it does no good to go out and shake one's fist at the storm; it is safer to remain quietly indoors until the storm blows over.

Dionysius the Elder advised, "Let thy speech be better than silence; or be silent."

Someone has wisely declared, "Well timed silence is more eloquent than speech."

"Peace has its victories," John Milton observed, "no less renowned than war."

New courage and power are instilled in the heart of a whole group when each individual determines to harbor and insist on a spirit of peace. In spite of a complexity of duties, the angels of heaven maintain an unbroken, happy, inspiring peace. And children of men, who are potential saints of glory, will eagerly pray for grace to live peaceably with all men.

The Bible tells us, "Strive for peace with all men." Fight for peace! Fight, not others, but ourselves, so that we may have peace with others. Look for those things in life to which most Christians agree. Emphasize the points of harmony. "Behold, how good and pleasant it is when brothers dwell in unity!"

Solomon, the wise man, said, "When a man's ways please the Lord, he makes even his enemies to be at peace with him."

At one time Luther received a complaint from one Christian against another Christian. Exclaimed Luther, "O God, help us! What a power the devil has received when he can make the Christians disagree, who ought rather to influence others to be agreeable, and to set a good example in peaceableness!"

The Superintendent of one of our Lutheran Hospitals was once invited to speak at the graduation of nurses at a Catholic Hospital. When the commencement program was completed, he was invited to eat lunch with a number of priests. At the table the priests were discussing their own religion, and then they asked him to tell about his faith. For a time they were all unusually friendly. But in his eagerness one of the younger priests started to insist that the Catholic viewpoint alone is correct. The priest kept pressing his point until the visitor, as well as others, became embarrassed. Then the Father Monsignor, who was sitting next to the visitor, pushed a bowl of sugar over to the enthusiastic priest and suggested, "Here, take some sugar and let it sweeten your words." The young priest had nothing more to say. Would it not be well if we all could take some kind of "sugar" to sweeten our thoughts and our words?

However desirable and valuable peace among men may be, justice and truth are still more precious. Truth and righteousness must never be sold out for peace. A Christian must still "contend for the faith." As long as he lives it is his privilege to "fight the good fight of the faith." Most of the time it is well to try to maintain peace at all costs. But there do come times when, to keep quiet is to betray one's God, one's faith, one's Church, one's family, and country.

Times will come when it is essential for a person to stand up and to speak out in love what he knows is right and honorable in the sight of God. Straight-forward, friendly and frank discussion clarifies the air and dispels many a disagreement and misunderstanding. Frank presentation of facts will often pave the way for enduring peace and harmony. In Christian experience there is the possibility of fighting peaceably.

Christians who are confronted by common problems ought to find it easy to get along with one another. Our quarreling only strengthens the cause of the enemy. But in marching along together, and working together peaceably for an ideal much greater than any personal rights or ambitions, we can well afford to permit God to create in our hearts an ever-increasing spirit of brotherly love and peace.

On the mountainous boundary between the two great South American republics, Chile and Argentina, there stands the heroic statue, the Christ of the Andes. It was erected by the two nations to symbolize their intention to remain at peace with each other. On the base one may read this inscription, "These mountains shall fall before the Chileans and Argentines break the peace that they have sworn at the feet of Christ the Redeemer."

Mankind has never discovered a more sensible solution for the problems of peace than the realization of the presence of Christ. In the constant presence of Christ it is difficult to fight, to quarrel, or think unkindly of anyone. The Christ of the Andes, and the Christ of the Storm, and the Christ of the Upper Room, challenges and enables His disciples to remain at peace among themselves.

Teach us to love each other, Lord,
As we are loved by Thee;
None who are truly born of God
Can live in enmity.

THOMAS COTTERILL.

Chapter IX

GOD, MY EXCEEDING JOY

TODAY many people repeat the heartfelt prayer of David, "Restore to me the joy of thy salvation." Like David, many have had blessed experiences of God's forbearance and providence, but they crave the renewed experience of an uplifting, abiding joy.

In spite of the error of his ways, David knew that he was still a child of God. Praying for mercy, he felt assured that God would forgive him, that God would have mercy upon him, and that God would give him a clean heart and a right spirit. But he wanted something more; he wanted to be happy in God.

At a former time David did have the assurance of being a child of God. Had he not, through faith in God, been enabled to conquer the defiant Goliath? Had he not conquered neighboring nations? But he could not conquer himself. Because of his fall into sin, David knew he was guilty before God. This sense of guilt made him fearful. His former gladness was overwhelmed by the bitterness in his soul. His assurance of salvation faded away into painful doubts.

Wisely David turned to God, for no one but God could restore to the deeper levels of his soul the inspiring and uplifting satisfaction of knowing that God cared for him. From previous experiences he felt certain that somehow God would be waiting to share with him a rich measure of His own abiding and sustaining joy.

73

The very fact that David prayed for mercy and forgiveness was an indication of the presence of the grace of God in his soul, even during the time when he felt sadness in his penitent heart. If he had completely fallen away from God, he would not have prayed for mercy.

If David tried to compel himself to be happy, his elation would be subject to human effort, personal behavior, and every whim of human error. But when he prayed that God would restore his joy, he was assured that such exultation would be genuine, heaven-sent and soul-sustaining.

From time to time David expressed his delight in God:

"I was glad when they said to me, Let us go to the house of the Lord!"

"But let all who take refuge in thee rejoice, let them ever sing for joy; and do thou defend them, that those who love thy name may exult in thee."

"This is the day which the Lord has made; let us rejoice and be glad in it."

"Thou dost show me the path of life; in thy presence there is fullness of joy, in thy right hand are pleasures for evermore."

"Serve the Lord with gladness."

In Psalm 43, King David prayed, "Oh send out thy light and thy truth; let them lead me, let them bring me to thy holy hill and to thy dwelling!" The holy hill, where the house of God was located, was good, but the hill itself could never satisfy his spiritual need.

"Let them bring me . . . to thy dwelling." The dwelling, the tabernacle, is better and closer, but the tabernacle, or attendance there alone, is not in itself enough.

"Then will I go to the altar of God." Just to make a gift of many animals on the altar of sacrifice could never produce peace or joy in David's heart. Or even to approach as close as he could to the ark of the covenant would not feed his soul. Above the ark was the Shekinah, the two angels symbolizing the presence of God, the glory of God. For his soul he needed something more than a symbol, something more than the altar.

David needed God as a personal possession, as his personal joy. Or rather, he needed to know that God possessed him. Only the sacrifice that God was making for David could satisfy his deepest thirst. Only as he would be certain that he could address God as "my" God would he find restful joy. In "God, my exceeding joy," alone could he become satisfied. Now he could rest his soul in God alone.

Thus David yearned to commune with God himself in the temple. In the divine worship he wanted to know God. In the Word of God and in the music he wanted to be convinced of the power and the grace of God to save him personally. In the moment of deepest need David felt a strong attraction to Him who alone could make his joy complete, abounding, and uplifting.

Basking in the sunshine of God's love, David was inspired as he experienced again the warming, cheering, strengthening rays of grace personally permeating his own heart and soul. In the constant presence of God he found the gracious restoration of true, heart-warming, abiding victory.

David indicated that God was not only his joy, but his "exceeding joy." There is no other rejoicing like it. Spurgeon declared, "God is, not only the fountain of joy, or the giver of joy, or the maintainer of joy, but joy itself." To draw near to God himself is to be enlightened by the glories of His eternal, personal blessedness.

For us, too, it is well that we go to church and even to the altar, but these alone are not enough. They are not ends in themselves, but only means to an end, a blessed means, however, leading to Him alone who is the best of all, "God, my exceeding joy."

75

Rejoicing in God exceeds all other delight, "in its nature, degree and duration. It is in the mercy, justice and love of God that the springs of real joy are found. And this joy is amplified and clarified from day to day in the assurance of the sustaining grace and providence of God to keep His trusting children unto a blessed victory."

REASONS FOR VICTORIOUS JOY

Many people are thwarted by a spirit of sadness and frustration. There is not a person anywhere but has felt the sting of some deep disappointment. But at the same time, regardless of his experience, every one has something for which to be ever deeply, wholeheartedly grateful to God. As children of the King, we have at all times God at our side. He leads the way. Time and again His guardian angels protect us.

One of the reasons for sadness is often unbelief. We trust in our inadequate wisdom rather than the tried, proven and perfect wisdom of God. Or, it may be some unforgiven sin. God cannot forgive sin that is cherished or retained. When a person turns to God in sincere repentance, asking God to forgive the sin that is confessed, and asking God to help him to do what is right, God will gladly forgive him. And then, and not until then, will God be more than happy to flood such a soul with a deep, sincere, abiding assurance of forgiveness. Confession gives working room for God. In Isaiah God says, "I am He who blots out your transgressions for my own sake, and I will not remember your sins."

In the desert of this world we do well to dig our spiritual wells very deep in order to tap the streams that flow from the City of God. In the storms of life, if we would seek a solid joy and a bouyant calm, we do well to build the sub-foundations of our faith deeply and securely on the solid Rock of Ages.

We never know real enjoyment except against the background of an experience of sorrow. Sorrow brings out the value of true joy. Against the background of black, heavy, rolling clouds, the multi-colored rainbow stands out in all its beauty. Amid the experience of trying disappointments, true bliss shines forth in all its hope-inspiring excellence. When the grace of God shines upon the penitent sinner with blessing, hope and forgiveness, then there dawns upon that person a realization of something of the beauty of God's far-reaching Providence.

True rejoicing is a sober and serene blessing springing from the heart of God. All the shadows of life are of man's making. All the blessings of our life are of God's making. Spiritual joy is one of the fruits of the Spirit. Spiritual satisfaction dwells, not on the tongue, but silently in the heart. This blessing cannot be described to us or to others; it must be personally experienced if we are to know its exceeding richness.

After the prophet Elijah had called down fire from heaven to consume his sacrifice, he ran away from the threatenings of wicked Queen Jezebel. In southern Arabia the prophet became discouraged because he felt that he was of no earthly use to himself, to Israel, or to God. Lonesome, he imagined that he was the only true believer left in the world. But then the Lord revealed to him that there were seven thousand faithful in Israel, and He also showed Elijah some important work He wanted him to do.

When Paul was in prison in Jerusalem his spirit no doubt at times ran quite low. What a strange reward, he might think, for faithfulness to Christ! Maybe he imagined that all his work had come to an end. But the Lord stood by him and said, "Take courage, for . . . you must bear witness also at Rome." This assurance of continued usefulness bouyed his spirit into a new vision of hopefulness and confidence.

Both Elijah and Paul became more contented when they realized that others were depending upon them to do their work faithfully. The Lord still had something vital for each of them to be doing. Both the people and the Lord needed them.

When Paul wrote to the churches, he did not complain about the faults of the people. He rather expressed confidence and gratitude because of the progress of God's work already made in and through them. If we, too, would only think for a minute of the former life and background of some of the friends with whom we work, and recall something of the spiritual growth that has already taken place, we would be filled with justifiable and encouraging delight.

REJOICING IN THE WORK OF THE LORD

Thank God for the marvelous growth of the gospel in the last nineteen centuries! The work is far from completed. So much remains to be done. And who are to see to it that the work of the Lord advances and expands, if not we who have experienced something of the grace of God!

Whoever we may be, there are some people who have been blessed, and still can be blessed, by our devotion to our duty. More people than we first realize will be immeasurably helped, both directly and indirectly, if we assume or re-assume wholeheartedly and zealously the work which the Lord has laid out for us.

Somebody will go astray if we do not do our duty today. And who knows but that our most important work under God lies ahead of us? Only God knows the increasing measure of encouragement that He has prepared for us in the days that are to come. If we walk with Christ, it is promised us, "You shall see greater things than these."

Personally we are not important, but the work of the Lord

is important. The gospel is important. And souls are important. For their sake, for the sake of the Lord and for our own sake, we shall look to our Redeemer for the grace necessary to carry on as long as the Lord needs us. Soon enough will come the summons, "Enter into the joy of your master."

What greater exultation can there be than in sharing with someone else some Word of God! It may be in some Sunday School class, or in a private conversation. God has given us the definite promise that His Word, which we ourselves speak, or someone else speaks, or which we help someone to speak, is not going to return void. It is sure to accomplish God's gracious purposes.

Occasionally someone may express a word of appreciation for something we may say to them or do for them; but whether people say anything or not, we can enjoy the comfort of knowing that God's Word is taking root, growing and bearing fruit in the lives of many more than we may imagine.

What a thrill filled the heart of one Christian who received a note from a former member of his Sunday School class. His friend wrote, "If it were not for you, I would not have known Jesus Christ, our Savior! Every morning as I kneel down before God to pray, I think of you."

Even though some person may not be consciously converted or spiritually awakened at every service which we attend or help to support, we do have the assurance that the Word of God is adding to the sum total of religious experience of the people who hear or read it. When people hear the Word of God, at least those who are attentive are being built up in their most holy faith.

Every Christian shares in the satisfaction of knowing that his part in the work bears definite relationship to each worshiper's growth in the grace and knowledge of Christ.

Through our presence, our prayers, our gifts of love, our labors, plus the blessing of God, we all enjoy a share of the privilege of bringing souls closer to Christ.

Bishop Cyprian once wrote to his friend Donatus, "This is a cheerful world as I see it from my garden, under the shadow of my vines. But if I could ascend some high mountain and look out over the wide lands, you know very well what I should see: brigands on the highways, pirates on the seas, armies fighting, cities burning; in the amphitheatres men murdered to please applauding crowds, selfishness and cruelty and misery and despair under all roofs. It is a bad world, Donatus, an incredibly bad world.

"But I have discovered in the midst of it a quiet and holy people, who have learned a great secret. They have found a joy which is a thousand times better than any of the pleasures of our sinful life. They are despised and persecuted, but they care not. They are masters of their souls. They have overcome the world. These people, Donatus, are the Christians, and I am one of them."

How the Coming of Christ Brought Joy

There is no more reliable source of deep joy than the life of Christ. It was because God wanted to restore to His yearning people a full measure of true delight that He sent His Son into the world. The coming of Christ was intended to bring "Joy to the World." His birth brought "good news of a great joy." Many of His people sing,

> "Oh, the precious Name of Jesus,
> How it thrills our souls with joy."

He who is the "Hope of earth and Joy of heaven," wants His people to receive a full measure of His abounding blessing. In the very shadow of the cross Christ spoke of His own deep, abiding, sustaining joy. He prayed that His disciples might be filled with and radiate His own plentiful, heaven-born contentment.

The Man of Sorrows found one of the deep sources of His victorious rejoicing in the happy assurance that He was indeed the well-beloved Son of His heavenly Father. Enemies ridiculed Him. Friends underestimated Him. But when the voice from heaven said, "This is My beloved Son," that was all that mattered to Him.

Jesus was happy in His Father. He was always aware of what His Father was doing for Him. Wherever He went, whatever He might say, He was always thinking of His Father. Even though He lived on earth, He testified that He was "in heaven." The whims and cruelties of men could never disturb the sources of His supreme conquest over Satan and the world. Our Lord was sustained and inspired by a deep, mysterious comfort that the world can never comprehend.

Jesus' exultation was constant because He trusted implicitly in the promises of His Father. Living close to His Father, He enjoyed victorious hope in the future expansion of His Kingdom. Everything that Jesus said or did was planned to give solid happiness to His followers and to their offspring for generations to come.

As we study the parables of Jesus, we observe what enjoyment He found in nature. Our Lord compared the blessings of the Kingdom with the happiness of harvest, or of possessing a treasure, a pearl, or a coin. Every soul, like that of Zaccheus, that returned to God was cause for His rejoicing. The repentance of one convert, He said, amplifies the exultation in heaven. Every indication of growth of faith or holiness among His disciples was an occasion of rejoicing in His heart.

When Christ sowed the Seed of the Word, He did not complain because much of His message would be lost.

Rather He was happy in the assurance that it would enter deep into the good soil of at least some sincere hearts and would grow up and bear fruit in unselfish service for others. When He spoke of the tares being mixed with the wheat He was joyously confident that every "grain of wheat" would be kept safe for eternity.

The Lord was always confident of the ultimate victory of right over wrong, of truth over falsehood. Because of the joy set before Him, He was given grace to endure the cross and on Easter to be raised from the dead. His soul was unconquerable for He depended, not on what men said, but on what God said. The severest testings and the hardest trials only proved that His spiritual contentment was genuinely sincere and invulnerable. Even the anguish of Gethsemane blossomed into the joys of Easter and the ascension.

In going about doing good Jesus discovered fresh, daily delight. Thinking seldom of His own needs, and being saved from the blight of greed, His heart and life were made buoyantly happy in unselfishly making others happy.

In associating with tried friends, such as Martha and Mary and Lazarus, Jesus thoroughly enjoyed Himself. He took part in social functions, attended weddings and feasts, and always contributed something to the happiness of others.

Many of Jesus' words were aimed to fill His listeners with gladness. To the man sick of the palsy He said, "Be of good cheer," or, "Take heart, my son, your sins are forgiven."

Even, though His followers should be reviled and persecuted for His sake, Jesus said to them, "Rejoice and be glad, for your reward is great in heaven."

At another time Christ declared, "These things I have spoken to you, that my joy may be in you, and that your joy may be full." "I will see you again and your hearts will rejoice, and no one will take your joy from you." "Rejoice because your names are written in heaven."

In the Beatitudes Christ pointed out to the multitudes many reasons for rejoicing. Because of His insight into the deeper purposes of circumstances, Christ could explain that in the midst of the people's most troublesome problems they still had a rare, eternal opportunity to appropriate for themselves the most valuable and genuine comforts of life.

Sooner or later every person is confronted by many a mountainous problem. But when those difficulties are brought before God in earnest prayer, a person discovers that they are really an opportunity through which God wants to give such a person a supreme blessing. God does not want to take anything away from His people; in truth, He wants to give them a rich experience of His sustaining grace.

God desires to teach His beloved people enduring lessons in gratitude, strength and victorious assurance. Even in their mourning, or spiritual poverty, or hungering or thirsting for righteousness, or whatever it might be, Christ insisted that His listeners had marvelous opportunities for rejoicing.

Suffering burns away the dross and qualifies a person for sustaining satisfactions. It is only through many sorrows and testings of faith that a Christian attains the gentleness, Christian understanding, and sense of deep gratitude essential for true Christian living.

What greater delight can a person have than to be a branch in Christ, the Vine! There a person finds invisible but real sustenance. Whether the branches are in full foliage, or heavy with grapes, or bare, or in full length, or pruned ever so short, all that really matters is whether or not the branch is still dependent upon the Vine. In every kind of "weather" there will be grace sufficient for each

83

trial. Such rejoicing arises from the deep secret of spiritual satisfactions in Christ.

As people live in Christ, they miraculously absorb some of His Spirit and His joy. When people devote themselves most wholeheartedly to the honor of Christ, they will be walking in the Way which yields the richest rejoicings. We cannot safely rejoice in the world, or in ourselves, or in others. But we can confidently "rejoice in the Lord."

Is not our experience something like that of the Ethiopian eunuch? As he was riding along in his chariot he was reading the fifty-third chapter of Isaiah, but did not understand the meaning.

Along came Philip who "told him the good news of Jesus." The Ethiopian then understood the passage, accepted Christ as his personal Savior, was baptized, and "went on his way rejoicing."

Philip, no doubt, after he had led the Ethiopian to Christ, also went on his way rejoicing.

> But I look up—into the face of Jesus,
>   For there my heart can rest, my fears are stilled;
> And there is joy, and love, and light for darkness,
>   And perfect peace, and every hope fulfilled.

ANNIE JOHNSON FLINT.

84

Chapter X

CONTRIBUTING TO THE HAPPINESS OF OTHERS

ALICE FREEMAN PALMER, onetime president of Wellesley College, seemed always to be beaming with a happiness which started ever-widening circles of cheerfulness wherever she went. Asked one day how she could be so happy all the time, Mrs. Palmer said, "Yes, I will tell you. I will give you three simple rules. Obey them, practice them, and you, too, will be happy.

"The first rule is this: Commit something to memory every day, something good. It need not be much, just a bit of a poem, or a Bible verse; three or four words will do.

"The second rule is: Look for something beautiful every day—if not beautiful, at least something pretty.

"My third rule is—Do something for somebody every day. It need not be a great thing, but do something for somebody other than yourself. This is the secret."

In the lives of many people happiness is an evasive blessing. People want to be happy, but cheerfulness for them is as elusive as trying to pick up a drop of mercury with one's fingers. Mozart lived and died in abject poverty, but he must have had a deep, personal joy in knowing that his talent would give future generations such exquisite melodies.

Beethoven began to be deaf at twenty-eight and toward the end of his life could not even hear his own symphonies. But he found real joy in contributing to lovers of good music echoes of heavenly melodies which kept ringing in his mind.

At forty-six Pasteur was crippled by a paralytic stroke; all through life he fought heavy odds. Time and again the dull stupidity of men of his day blocked him. But think of the quiet joy that was his in knowing that many people would live, and live better, because of his patient pioneering!

Lincoln walked a sorrowful way, troubled, tormented. Time and again he was threatened with violence. But he was thrilled by an inner joy, knowing that he had emancipated a nation within a nation, and had united his native land.

Robert Louis Stevenson was sickly most of his life. Other people in his circumstances would have been very unhappy. But Stevenson, sustained by a victorious faith, said, "I believe in the ultimate decency of things; aye, and if I woke up in hell, I should still believe it."

It seems strange that so many lives seem to be handicapped by frustration, calamity, and tragedy. But God is good, who encourages His children to seek joy, not in pleasure, but in Him. God wants everyone to learn that earthly happiness is fleeting and undependable, and that the only enjoyment worth while is that which is found when people resign themselves into His hands and become agents for bringing God's good plans for humanity into a blessed reality.

There are some Christians whose many trials hide the joy in their hearts. Their joy seldom finds expression in outward cheerfulness. Others misunderstand them because their faces do not always reflect the joyous emotion in their hearts. It is easy to be outwardly happy when everyone else is happy and when circumstances are favorable. But when trials come and "sorrows like sea-billows roll," a person is indeed fortunate, if he has learned to drink deeply from the eternal well-springs of God's joy.

When things seem discouraging, it is well to recall that

the Kingdom of God is gaining new converts every day and will make still greater conquests in the future. Friends and relatives may pass away, property may be lost, nations may be overthrown, but we know that in spite of all, Christ is still our Friend and Brother, and sooner than we expect, will be revealed as victorious Conqueror in the lives of many.

So often we look forward to some great rejoicing in the future or wish that we were some other place, or in someone else's place. So often we fail to see reasons for heartfelt gratitude and uplifting pleasure in our very midst. We toil and slave to overtake some fleeting delight and overlook the rich blessings available every day.

Every commonplace event and every simple thing about us is bursting at the seams, so to say, with a wealth of enjoyment, if we only have the vision to discern it. Do we not have friends who are sincerely interested in our welfare? What is more enjoyable than taking the family, or a few real friends, or even to go by oneself, for a hike into the woods, or on a trip to some park, or river, or lake? Even but a few moments' conversation with a friend on the street, or over the back fence, or with a circle of friends in one's own parlor, or at a sick-bed, is a privilege not to be scorned.

Think how many beautiful things there are in the world! Active exercise in the open air is a bracing tonic for anyone. To observe and to listen to nature, to live the simple, useful, dignified life is happiness supreme. To be independent of luxuries gives a person sustaining satisfaction.

Then there is the sincere uplift of the friendly song of a robin or a meadow lark, the majesty of an awe-inspiring sunset, the healing power of rolling hills, the delicate mystery of a beautiful flower, the smile of a tiny baby. Real are the pleasures to be discovered in reading a good book or an outstanding magazine. And what is so satisfying and energizing as a few unhurried moments with the Bible! He is happiest whose work keeps him so occupied that he has to scheme and plot to secure even a small share of the pleasures of relaxation.

Inner happiness is independent of circumstances. A poor man can enjoy a good book as much as a millionaire. A workman may enjoy his simple fare more heartily than the rich man who picks at his choicest delicacies. A ragged boy with a home-made fish pole may get more real pleasure than a sportsman who is lavishly equipped. The beauties of spring, summer, autumn or winter are just as thrilling to a schoolgirl as to a fashionable debutante. And the members of a sandlot team can get more real enjoyment out of a game than all the spectators in the most expensive boxes in the big league park. Enjoyment comes, then, not so much from observing others, as in personal participation.

In his drama, "The Blue Bird," Maurice Maeterlinck has effectively interpreted man's eternal quest for happiness. Far and wide the little girl and boy, Mytyl and Tyltyl, sought for the blue bird of cheerfulness. They looked far into the future. They gazed into the sky. They searched in distant lands. But they hunted too far and too high.

Wearily returning home, they discovered the blue bird in their own yard. But having caught it, their happiness was not complete until they let it go free again. For joy cannot be kept for oneself; it must be shared with others.

A selfish person can never become happy; he only makes himself, and others, miserable. The unhappiest person is he who lives only for himself. Only he who, like Christ, lives for others, and delights in contributing to their happiness, knows the meaning of real happiness.

The soul that perpetually overflows with kindness and helpfulness to others is always radiating cheerfulness. The way to multiply one's own blessings is to share them with others.

He is most happy who can learn to be happy over the successes and blessings which come to other people. He who is happy over the successes and good fortunes of his fellow men will be spared from common envy and jealousy. There are always some Christians who are doing an outstanding work, and we can be happy when Christ is making progress through their labors of love.

When we forget ourselves, doing the things we know God wants us to be doing, always seeking the true welfare of others, we shall find happiness pursuing and surprising us at most unexpected occasions. Gladness does not come to us on a silver platter, like a roast turkey, but comes unbidden when we are busy with other things.

For years some people seem to labor with patient hope, often in drudgery, sadness and privation. But at last comes a notable day or a precious hour whose joy is so supreme and overwhelming that all the years of toil and waiting are more than amply repaid.

One day after Thomas A. Edison had worked for ten years perfecting the storage battery, someone asked him why he had worked so long and so hard. Edison replied, "I never worked a day in my life. It was all play." In his daily work Edison found his greatest happiness, making something useful for others around the world.

"There is no fun like hard work," someone has said.

Carlyle flung out the good invitation, "O, give us the man who sings at his work!" Carlyle also said, "The cheerful man will do more work in the same time, will do it better, and will persevere in it longer than anyone else." Thank God for work, not only for what it does for others, but what it does for us, mentally, spiritually, and physically!

One of Haydn's friends inquired of him how it happened

that his church music was usually of a cheerful and triumphant quality. Replied the great composer, "I cannot make it otherwise. I write according to the thoughts I feel. When I think about God, my heart is so full of joy that notes dance and leap, as it were, from my pen. And since God has given me a cheerful heart it will be easily forgiven me when I serve Him with a cheerful spirit."

HAPPINESS RECOMMENDS CHRISTIANITY

A happy Christian is a living recommendation for his religion. A Christian who radiates the deep, inner joy of the Savior is a great asset to his friends and associates. Such a person is a mighty inspiration for the cause of Christ. He wields an untold power for the spread of Christianity. Directly and indirectly, he convinces many of the genuine blessings to be found in the gospels. A happy man proclaims to the world that he serves a good Master. To serve Christ is the greatest enjoyment.

An increase in the number of people who reveal a cheerful attitude would be a welcome blessing among mankind. People respond to radiant cheerfulness. The Wise Man of the Bible wrote, "A glad heart makes a cheerful countenance." "A cheerful heart is a good medicine." A cheerful attitude transforms the meanest hut into a palace, a frugal lunch into a sumptuous banquet, a dire calamity into a rich blessing, and the hard road into an enjoyable boulevard. "Don't try to make yourself happy; just let yourself be happy."

Just to be happy starts countless ever-widening circles of happiness wherever one goes. A person who enjoys the blessings of God owes it to his fellow men to permit those blessings to be reflected in his face and in his voice and thus to spread around the aura of cheerfulness.

90

One of the debts we owe to others around us is a sincere, sunny smile. Just think how the spiritual wealth and mental health of the world could be improved a thousand-fold merely by the radiating and transforming power of buoyant contentment!

Frequently we ask the Lord to forgive us for our sinfulness, but ought we not also ask Him to forgive us for our unwarranted sadness? It is wrong for us to be sad, when God has given us every reason to rejoice evermore. God intended that His children should be not monuments of sorrow and despair, but radiant lights beaming with dependable and increasing cheerfulness and gaiety.

Lights are made in order to dissipate darkness, to shine on what we want to see. A Christian is redeemed and sent forth as a lamp to brighten man's pathway, to help light man's way to God.

Those who have experienced many trials of their own can better convince others of the sustaining power of God's grace and joy. A person in whose heart Christ makes His home will manifest, not only a spirit of contagious faith and power, but contagious happiness as well.

How refreshing and happy we become when we enter into the company of delightful and cheerful people! As Christians, we have every reason for spreading rays of sunshine and an atmosphere of exhilaration wherever we go. Every time a person spreads happiness to others about him he adds something wholesome and invigorating to his own life as well.

Even the most beautiful cities occasionally experience dismal, dreary days. A day might be ever so foggy, stormy and gloomy in old Boston, but when Phillips Brooks walked down one of its narrow, winding streets, speaking a cheery word here, or waving a cheerful greeting to someone across the street, radiating, wherever he went, a buoyant, infectious happiness, the street was transformed.

Brooks had his problems, the same as anyone else. He was not always smiling, but he was ready at an instant's notice for a smile. And it was not just an ordinary smile, for he smiled with his eyes, as well as with his whole personality. Because he lived close to God, and because he knew he was a child of the King, Phillips Brooks exemplified that noble army of encouraging souls who leave behind them a trail of sunny cheerfulness and inspiring hopefulness.

"Hallelujah! for the Lord our God, the Almighty reigns. Let us rejoice and exult and give him the glory."

Chapter XI

I AM NOT WORTHY

WHEN a person stands and looks up at a near-by, mighty mountain he begins to realize how relatively small he really is. When he stands on the shore and looks out over the wide, and deep, and far-flung ocean he feels quite insignificant. Or, when at night, he reverently gazes up into the brilliant, limitless, starry universe, he keenly feels his own limitations.

"A mountain may laugh at a molehill until both begin to look up to the stars."

In the crisis of a serious illness a patient realizes how utterly helpless and weak he may become. In the presence of an eminent personality a person should be respectful. As thoughtful Lincoln would quote, "Why should the spirit of mortal be proud?"

Possibly some of us may be honest enough to make the confession of a five year old boy who declared, "I suppose I seem bigger to myself than I really am." The Bible warns us against thinking more highly of ourselves than we ought to think. Emerson observed, "We are all needed, but none of us very much."

The Struggle Between Pride and Humility

Humility and pride wage a life-long struggle. "It was pride," Augustine observed, "that changed angels into demons; it is humility that makes men into saints." Our worst, secret enemy is our own pride. Pride cannot be

93

driven out by laws or rules, for pride will not submit to rules. The pride of one person will not drive out pride from someone else, for Satan does not drive out himself.

The proud heart cannot know the love of God, nor can it rightly become acquainted with itself. To hide his shortcomings, a careless or inefficient workman often resorts to an air of superiority. A self-important person is more likely to give frequent vent to outbursts of temper, for an egotistic person is much more easily offended than one who is humble.

An overabundant self-confidence is sure to send a person down to eventual certain defeat. Self-importance and arrogance are sure to suffer a fall, and the sooner it comes, the better for all concerned. Nothing is so offensive as pretended or affected humility which is only another manifestation of pride.

One of the roots of all our big mistakes is pride. A proud person is unwilling to learn the truth about himself. He is unwilling to foresee the blessings of humble obedience. Joseph Fort Newton came one day to a town to give an address. A friend of his drove him around to show Newton the city. As they rode along the friend pointed out where several firms had once carried on their businesses, but now they had failed.

"Why did they fail?" inquired Newton. "It may surprise you, perhaps," the friend replied, "but they failed for a religious reason. They lacked humility."

Then the friend went on to point out that these firms had prided themselves on past successes. They were unwilling to see or to admit their weaknesses. Nor were they willing to learn new methods, to keep up to date, or to improve their services to their clientele. So they failed. Their pride was their undoing.

The great poet of the ancient church, the Spaniard Prudentius, wrote, "You may have power and riches, wisdom and beauty, but pride alone will destroy everything, if it is harbored." Pride has brought the downfall of many individuals, families, congregations, institutions, and nations. "Therefore let any one who thinks that he stands take heed lest he fall."

One of the common manifestations of pride is the delusion that, because a person may be an expert in one occupation, he is thereby qualified to speak with authority concerning everybody else's business. A humble person realizes his own limitations and is willing to learn from others. He understands that he does not know the last word about his own occupation; how then can he speak with authority about the labors of others?

Usually it takes a lifetime for a person to learn fully about his own occupation. It has taken everyone else likewise a lifetime of experience and study to acquire what he knows. We do well to respect the knowledge and experience of others.

When a person begins to investigate all the information filed away in a large library, or to look through the catalog of a large college or university, he begins to appreciate how little he really knows of the vast fund of human knowledge. And besides this is the vast store of scientific data and experience not yet discovered.

How wisely J. H. Newman saw his own life:

"I loved to choose and see my path,
    And spite of fears,
    Pride ruled my will."

Many people have lost their vaunted pride in the service of Him who was willing to be considered the least of all. The life and death of Jesus Christ are a standing rebuke to every form of human pride. They who best know Christ cannot help but be humble. They who really know themselves have every reason to be sober-minded. In the constant presence of Christ, a person should be very lowly.

Young grain growing in the field stands erect. But as the grains of wheat develop and gain weight the heads bow low as they sway in the wind. People of inexperience can strut about with their heads high. But as trials and experience develop soundness of soul, heads become willing to bow low under the burden of gratitude for all of God's blessings.

HUMILITY REVEALS THE MAJESTY OF GOD

"Humility, like darkness," Thoreau observed, "reveals the heavenly lights." From the standpoint of lowliness we learn best how to trust in God. God walks with the humble of heart. Not to the wise and understanding, but to the lowly in heart, God reveals His special grace. James Stewart has said, "Only when we strike rock bottom in our own nothingness, will we strike the Rock of Ages."

Nothing places a person in a position where he can receive the blessings of God like humility, and nothing sets a person out of the reach of Satan so much as genuine modesty. True submissiveness paves the way for the progress of the Spirit of Christ.

It is strange to notice that of all the virtues and blessings which people seek today, meekness is often forgotten. Men desire greater possessions, or promotions, or honors, which often lead to pride and aloofness from the needs of the common people. But very few have grace to seek the submissiveness which leads to lasting, genuine, final exaltation from the hand of God himself.

A humble man knows how far he is from what he ought to be. For that reason he is willing to learn, and to grow, and to make constant improvements. Tolstoi was aware of his distance from his ideal, and it made him humble. He knew that in some ways he possessed greater abilities than many others, but he never boasted about them.

Truly good men are never heroes to themselves. They realize how much farther they should have advanced. A humble person desires to do his very best, but having done it, he is still humble, because he knows that in the sight of God he is only an unprofitable servant.

Humility is a Christian blessing of extraordinary beauty. All people, even the ungodly, admire a person who is genuinely unaffected, non-pompous, unassuming, self-effacing, and willing to accept his rightful share of a common load. A modest appraisal of one's ability is a prime necessity for usefulness.

There is nothing so admirable in a Christian as growth in the beauty of submission to Christ. If we want to be more dedicated disciples of our Lord, who was meek and lowly, we can do no better than to let Christ live out His humility through us.

He who wants to be a true Christian is never exalted because of his abilities, or influence, or successes. He lives in the fear of God and keeps in mind the day of final reckoning when he shall have to give account for the use and development of his God-given powers.

Humbled, Jacob prayed, "I am not worthy of the least of all the steadfast love and all the faithfulness which thou hast shown to thy servant." John the Baptist was truly a humble man. When he spoke of his relationship to Christ he testified of Christ as one "whose sandals I am not worthy to carry." One day in Capernaum there came to our Lord a centurion who had a servant who was sick. He said to Him, "Lord, I am not worthy to have you come under my roof." And yet the Lord said that this centurion had more faith than anyone in Israel. When the prodigal son returned home he confessed to his father, "I have sinned; I am no longer worthy to be called your son."

"It is from out of the depths of humility," said M. Mountford, "that the height of our destiny looks grandest. Let me truly feel that in myself I am nothing, and at once, through every inlet of my soul, God comes in, and is everything to me."

Humility Accepts All Things as from God

Once there was a man who, though highly gifted, was willing to work in a situation where very few people seemed to appreciate his efforts. One day as he was walking along with a friend, the friend asked him why he was wasting his time in such an insignificant place. The gifted man pointed to a spring of water, and said, "This fountain distinguishes itself in that it pours out its water, night and day, year after year, summer and winter, whether there are many or few who drink from it."

Whether there are many or few who appreciate his efforts, a child of God continues to do his work under the guidance of God because he knows that God will use his testimony and his work for the blessing of many needy souls.

When a man knows himself to be nothing, God can begin to use him. "A person who wants to be something great," John Arndt asserted, "is the substance of which God can make nothing, yea, of which he makes fools. But a person who is willing to be nothing and considers himself a nobody is the substance of which God can make something. Of such He makes glorious and wise men for His service."

"I appraise no one according to the greatness of his ability but according to his humility," said a certain Pastor Harris of England. "For it is not the keenest thinkers and the most learned men who bring the most people to Christian faith; it is the humblest."

98

Henry Schartau, one-time pastor in Lund, Sweden, said, "Humble yourself before God in a true repentance before He humbles you through suffering."

Rowland Hill, an English clergyman, said, "In the valley of *humility* a Christian is scot-free from the darts of the evil one, for this is the only place where the darts cannot penetrate and take hold."

Although Robert M. McCheyne of Scotland possessed extraordinary talents, he was said to have had such an exceptional humility that his equal has seldom been found in the history of the church.

J. Hudson Taylor, well-known founder and leader of the large China Inland Mission, possessed an uncommon humility which made a deep impression on his associates. One of his friends spoke to him of the remarkable development of his missionary projects.

With trembling lips Taylor testified, "I have sometimes thought that God must have looked around in different lands to find someone who was weak enough for such work, so that he could not take any honor unto himself. When God found the one He sought, He said, 'He is weak enough; he shall do this work.' All of God's giants have been weak men who did great things for God because they reckoned on His being with them."

Writing to a young Christian, who after some years of service still found himself in an obscure place and was becoming impatient for the recognitions of life, Professor David Smith wrote, "I will bless God daily for the long years which I spent in a remote corner of Scotland, working in a little village. It was oftentimes a disheartening experience, but it did me much good. True and abiding influence is slowly won and there is no more precious experience for youth than a protracted season of obscurity."

The quiet, obscure years, with their constant discipline of

heart and mind, are often the most enriching in a person's life. Many of the people who have performed great and good things first made their preparations and laid the foundations for their accomplishments in the quiet and humble places of service.

Over an old rectory garden door at Linton in Devonshire may be found this motto, "Live Unknown." It is the unknown soldiers of the cross, who in every generation, have borne the brunt of the burden, and without their devotion and sacrifices prominent men could never have performed their mighty deeds in the Lord. Yet all is done we trust, by humble and prominent alike, for the greater glory of God.

"Be content to go on working in obscurity a little longer," John Ruskin wrote to a young artist impatient for recognition. "There must be a seedtime of discipline and a quiet inner growth before there can be a harvest of experience and influence. It is better to let humility run its full course."

It is preferable for a person to be unrecognized than to receive honors that are undeserved or to receive honors that should have been given to others. What God wants is men great enough to be small enough to become thoroughly prepared for the hard tasks that lie ahead.

During his long life Thomas à Kempis remained loyal to his personal motto, "Love, and desire to be unknown." God has signally honored this servant of His. It is as though God wanted to set forth this humble, self-denying man for all subsequent centuries as an affirmation of the truth that "he who humbles himself shall be exalted."

For a long time the public did not know that à Kempis was the author of the famous book *The Imitation of Christ*. Many times he copied the book but always signed his name only as a copyist. Someone has said, "The obscurity of the author is one of the beautiful virtues of this book."

Now a long scientific research has definitely determined

100

that the author is none other than à Kempis himself. *The Imitation of Christ* has been published in over two thousand Latin editions, in about a thousand French editions, as well as in most of the living languages. Such is the blessing of a man who desired to be supremely devoted to his God, and preferred to let God have all the glory.

A person cannot make himself humble. Humility is a gift from God which He bestows upon those who yield themselves completely to Christ. The humble man does not rebel against the grace of God, but accepts everything as from the hand of God, as an occasion of spiritual opportunity. When a person confesses his own pride, God will help him to become truly humble.

If a humble person lacks ability, or makes mistakes, he will be the first to confess it. He will not boast of something he cannot do. But for anyone to pretend that he cannot do what he has the ability to do is not modesty, but disobedience. It is the sin of the unused talent.

THE HUMBLE MAN ACCEPTS GOD'S CHOICES

Through prayer and observation a humble person comes to a right estimate of his own God-given abilities. He becomes willing to accept God's choices for his life. "I have never been modest," Paderewski asserted, "because modesty is undervaluation. But I was humble, and I am still humble." Paderewski realized that by the grace of God he had been given the talent of an increasing measure of service to his fellow men. He became willing to dedicate his life to the accomplishment of any task for which his abilities suited him.

When Mary was told that she was to become the mother of Jesus she did not rebel. She was humbly willing to become and to do whatever God wanted of her. "Let it be to me," said Mary, "according to your word." Joseph likewise, thinking to put Mary away, saw a vision and was told the significance of his share in the coming of the Lord to the world. Joseph left the choice with God, and obeyed Him. Thank God for all who, giving up their own personal ambitions, find higher joy in doing God's will!

What does a person have that has not been given to him by the Lord? What can a person do which God has not helped him to do? Thank God for the people who are doing what they are doing, in the place where they are, because they know that God wants them there! They have learned to pray, "Lord, what do you want me to do in this situation? What would You do if You were in my place, here and now?" "God always gives the very best to those who leave the choice with Him!"

Tennyson related that *Crossing the Bar* flashed into his mind, perfect. He did not write it himself; it was written through him. He made no alterations. He lent his genius to be used by Another. Since Tennyson was yielded to God, God could use him. Notice his humble confession:

> "And in me there dwells
> No greatness, save it be some far-off touch
> Of greatness to know well
> I am not great."

Joseph Fort Newton once related the story of a man who had a deep spiritual experience. The man wrote him, "At one time in my life, years ago, I was addicted to drink. Not a sot, but a man well saturated with whiskey. I did not like the whiskey, but I did like and need the effect.

"Then one day, just how or why I do not know, I dropped it, cut it out entirely, and have not touched it since. I did not take a vow; I was not about to go down over the dam. But, somehow, Something, or Someone, seemed to take the

102

glass out of my hand. That is all I can say about it—it is as much a mystery to me as to anyone else."

Robert Louis Stevenson related a somewhat similar spiritual experience. "I can remember a time," he wrote, "when I was very idle. I have no idea why I ceased to be so. Of the great change which decided all the later part of my life, turning me from one whose business it was to shirk into one whose business it is to strive and persevere, I can say only this: All the work seems to have been done by Someone Else. I was never conscious of a struggle. I never registered a vow. I merely 'came about' like a well-handled ship. There stood at the wheel that Unknown Steersman we call God."

F. B. Meyer, noted Bible student of England once said, "I used to think that God's gifts were on shelves one above the other, and that the taller we grow in Christian character the more easily we should reach them. I find now that God's gifts are on shelves one beneath the other, and that it is not a question of growing taller, but of stooping lower, and that we have to go down, always down, to get His best gifts."

Give me the lowest place;
Not that I dare ask for the lowest place,
But Thou hast died that I might live,
And share Thy glory by Thy side.

Give me the lowest place;
Or if for me, that lowest place too high,
Make one more low where I may sit
And see my God and love Thee so!

CHRISTINA ROSSETTI.

Chapter XII

GIVING CREDIT TO OTHERS

W ILLIAM S. KNUDSEN was at one time an executive, first with Ford Motor Company, and then with Chevrolet Motor Company. On the occasion of the sixtieth birthday anniversary of Mr. Knudsen, leading business and professional men honored him at a banquet in Detroit. Speakers extolled the remarkable success of the onetime immigrant boy who had become one of the outstanding business leaders of the nation. In the simple humility which often accompanies true greatness, Mr. Knudsen responded, "Whatever I have done and whatever I have received in life has been due to the men who have helped me."

A humble person considers other people better than himself. He is not jealous or envious because of the abilities or the good fortunes of others. He trains himself to be contented wherever he is and to make still better use of his own talents and opportunities.

A person honors himself when he gives due credit to others because of their abilities and achievements. We are fools if we take to ourselves credit that rightly belongs to others. We have entered into a work which others before us have prepared, and others around us are carrying on with considerable labor and sacrifice.

When Colonel Charles A. Lindbergh returned from his "Lone Eagle" flight across the Atlantic he was enthusiastically feted throughout the nation. Although speakers praised him without measure, the feature of his personality that stirred the admiration of the throngs was his simple humility. Time after time he straight-forwardly asserted that he could not have made his flight if it had not been for the many pioneers, inventors, mechanics, and others who had prepared the way for him. Lindbergh gave full credit to his predecessors and friends who had helped him directly and indirectly.

At the celebration held on the steps of the Capitol in honor of the one hundred fiftieth anniversary of the American flag, Charles Evans Hughes presented Lindbergh with a medal of honor. In his response Lindbergh said that credit for the flight should go, not so much to him, as to the many scientists and experimenters who had made the flight possible.

Lindbergh recalled that for centuries scientific designs and experiments had been made in trying to put together a flying machine. He also reminded his listeners of the previous twenty years of intensive research and widespread experimentation in which others had worked, and which now culminated in the construction of the airplane which carried him across the Atlantic.

The humility of Martin Luther was beautifully manifested when he wrote to Johann Brenz, "You are in every respect greater than I." Concerning the sermons of Brenz, Luther said, "There is no one among present-day theologians who can explain and expound the Holy Scriptures like Brenz, and I often marvel at his spirit, while I despair of my own ability."

John Calvin once wrote to a friend of his, "I adjure you never to forget what a great man Luther is, and with what gifts he is endowed. Remember with what spiritual strength, with what unconquerable persistency, and with what great learning he has consecrated his life to honor the

105

Christ. Remember also how far and wide he has spread the gospel of salvation. As far as I am concerned I have often said, and repeat it again, that I shall not cease to regard him with highest esteem and acknowledge that he is a distinguished servant of God."

By such a glowing testimony Calvin revealed the beauty of his own humility.

> *Done to obey Thy laws,*
> *E'en servile labors shine:*
> *Hallowed is toil, if this the cause,*
> *The meanest work divine.*
>
> JOHN WESLEY.

Chapter XIII

GIVE GOD THE GLORY

BECAUSE of the high value of spiritual influence there is danger that a Christian may take to himself some of the credit for his work for the Lord. Christians are often called upon to assume leadership, to occupy positions of responsibility, or with the help of others, to accomplish some great program of extraordinary importance. How perilously easy it is for a person to want credit for what *the Lord* has accomplished through him and others! It is both amusing and abhorrent, as well as untrue, to speak of our own great abilities and accomplishments.

One Christian, for instance, a man of considerable ability and unquestioned spiritual character and influence, had the habit of speaking too much of his own ideas and his own labors. In the course of one address he mentioned himself in the form of "I," "my," "me," or "mine" no less than a hundred and thirty times. He meant well. But his listeners had difficulty in looking through the maze of human accomplishments to see the works and the glory of God. Are we not all more or less similarly addicted?

On the other hand are there not also countless influential people who during a lifetime of useful activity have not mentioned themselves at all, except possibly in relating their own shortcomings or difficulties? Like Paul, they have preferred to report what great things God has done, or what good others have accomplished. Such objectivity is highly desirable; such humility, truly commendable.

A person who knows God, and who also knows himself, makes his appearances in all humility, with no show or pretension. He does not select the best places for himself. Rather he is willing to take the lowest place. He is content to work faithfully in his own modest place of duty and privilege until the Lord says, "Friend, go up higher." Even then he hesitates until he is convinced that it is truly the Lord who is calling him.

There is a manner of letting one's light shine so that a person himself receives all the glory, and others who have helped, and God, are forgotten and are left unthanked. We recall how King Herod, at a great banquet in his honor, took all the praise to himself and did not give God the glory.

There is, however, a manner of obedience to God in all humility so that even when a person performs "mighty works in the Lord," not the worker, but the Lord rightly receives the praise and glory.

John the Baptist was willing to decrease so that Christ might increase. A Christian serves best in a subdued light so that Christ may shine forth in all His splendor.

If we blow our own trumpet, our friends will not hear the still, small voice. If we display ourselves, we hide the Lord. A vase should not be so attractive that it draws the focus of attention from the beauty of the flowers it contains. Even the best of Christians are only ordinary people who should let the focus of attention rest on Christ.

A telegraph boy takes no credit for the importance of the message he delivers. A Christian cannot claim as his the importance of the message he tries to proclaim. But if he is truly a Christian he cannot help but be vitally interested in the contents of his message because of his own personal experience.

It has been well said, "A saint is one through whom the Light shines." A humble person realizes that all his talents are a gift from God, and any praise he may receive belongs, not to him, but to God. In the daytime a window lets in the light, but it is not the real source of light. The window is only the channel through which the light comes from the sun. A Christian is a person in whom God is working and through whom He is shedding His light.

What a change came over Peter! Early in his discipleship he had considered himself better than the rest. He even tried to tell his Lord what to do. But in later years he became willing to be quiet and to listen to his Lord.

Only a transformed Peter could write, "Likewise you that are younger be subject to the elders. Clothe yourselves, all of you, with humility toward one another, for, 'God opposes the proud, but gives grace to the humble.' Humble yourselves therefore under the mighty hand of God, that in due time he may exalt you." In later life Peter became willing to labor so "that in everything Christ might be pre-eminent."

In his gospel John makes no mention of his own name. When compelled to speak of himself he wrote simply, "Another disciple," "The other disciple," "The disciple whom Jesus loved," or "One of the sons of Zebedee." John effectually hid himself so that people might see Jesus only.

How Christ Glorified His Father

The outstanding example of humility is our blessed Lord. On the last journey to Jerusalem the disciples were arguing which of them was the greatest. Almost in the shadow of Calvary, the enthusiastic topic of conversation was personal importance and honor.

After they came to the upper room, in order to teach them a lesson in humility, Christ, who is Lord of lords and King of kings, girded himself with a towel like a slave, and taking a basin of water stooped down and washed the feet of the disciples. It was after Jesus had washed their feet that He said, "I have given you an example."

Of himself Christ said, "I am gentle and lowly in heart." Concerning his Lord, Paul wrote, "Have this mind among yourselves, which you have in Christ Jesus, who, though he was in the form of God, did not count equality with God a thing to be grasped, but emptied himself, taking the form of a servant, being born in the likeness of men. And being found in human form he humbled himself and became obedient unto death, even death on a cross. Therefore God has highly exalted him and bestowed on him the name which is above every name, that at the name of Jesus every knee should bow, in heaven and on earth and under the earth, and every tongue confess that Jesus Christ is Lord, to the glory of God the Father."

So Christ, who is the greatest of all, died for those who are the least of all. He who is richest of all offered himself to save the poorest of all. He who is the holiest of all died for the chief of sinners. He who is set over all things in the highest lifts to glory those who have sunk the deepest.

Is not much of our life like a row of zeroes? One failure, one shortcoming, one weakness, after the other—zero, zero, zero (00,000,000). Without Christ, life accomplishes nothing. But at the head of all our zeroes stands a Figure who adds meaning and value to that which follows, (100,000,000).

Christ is the One who gives worth, strength, power, and accomplishment for each hour and day. With Him we can do all things. Or rather, when we are yielded to Him, He can do all things through us. To Him belongs all the glory.

Whatever thanks or honors a Christian receives, he gladly passes on to Christ who has enabled him. Someone once asked Charles Kingsley how he could write such excellent poetry. "I have a Friend," he modestly and gratefully replied.

110

A great chorus was once rehearsing the oratorio *The Messiah*. Week after week the singers had been working together, and now they had arrived for the final rehearsal. Each number was carefully rehearsed in order to achieve the full shade of conviction and expression. The singers put their whole soul into the rehearsal and sang for their own supreme, spiritual and musical enjoyment as though no one else would ever hear it.

After they had arrived at the climax of the majestic and soul-gripping words and melodies, the director stood silent, transformed, humbly exultant, listening to the soulful echoes of the masterpiece.

"Who am I?" he asked. "I am nobody! Who are you? You are nobody."

The atmosphere bristled with intense emotion. Then he continued, "It is Handel—he is everything! Everything!"

Throughout the world, throughout the centuries, there has been a countless host of God's children, living and laboring together under one great Spirit. Some are active as Christians in their own homes, or in their respective places of business, or on the farms, or in institutions of learning, or of charity. Yet all are working together in one great oratorio of spiritual purpose.

"Who are we? Nobody! Who is any of us? *Nobody!* We are nothing, absolutely *nothing!* Unprofitable servants! Unworthy! It is God Triune and Triumphant! He is everything! Everything!"

Praise to the Lord! O let all that is in me adore Him!
All that hath life and breath, come now with praises before
  Him!
    Let the Amen
    Sound from His people again;
Gladly for aye we adore Him.

JOACHIM NEANDER.

111

Chapter XIV

LIVE AND HELP LIVE

AS SILAS MARNER played with his hoard of gold and let the coins fall through his open fingers, he imagined that he was having the time of his life. His gold was his god. Then his bags of gold were stolen, and the poor man imagined that life was no longer worth living. But actually it was the best thing that ever happened to him.

One day Silas Marner found in his home a little golden-haired girl. He learned to love the little girl, and took conscientious care of her. As the weeks and months rolled by, he provided for her hourly needs and discovered the real blessing of living. Getting his mind off himself and on someone else, he discovered the joy of helping others. Gratefully he learned that possessions are not an end in themselves, but only a means for making others happy.

One of the most helpful aspects of human experience is compassion for others. One of the significant characteristics of a true Christian is a Christ-like, all-embracing compassion. In Bunyan's *Pilgrim's Progress* one of the outstanding Christians is called Great-Heart. The original Great-heart is Christ himself. God's people also have the possibility of becoming helpful great-hearts.

All about us individuals cry out for someone to understand their needs, to care enough about them to listen to their pleas, and to be helpful in a practical, permanent manner. Was it not George Eliot who said in effect, "What do we live for, if it is not to make life more livable for others?"

112

THE COMPASSION OF JESUS

If there ever was one on earth who was compassionate and helpful, it was Jesus. It is said, "Jesus saw a great throng, and he had compassion on them, because they were like sheep without a shepherd." At another time, "he saw a great throng; and he had compassion on them, and healed their sick." Again, He said, "I have compassion on the crowd, because they have been with me now three days, and have nothing to eat; and I am unwilling to send them away hungry, lest they faint on the way."

The heart of Christ went out, not only to multitudes, but to individuals as well. For instance two blind men cried out as He passed by, and Jesus "in pity touched their eyes, and immediately they received their sight and followed him."

One day, as Christ approached the village of Nain, "a man who had died was being carried out, the only son of his mother, and she was a widow; and a large crowd from the city was with her. And when the Lord saw her, he had compassion on her and said to her, 'Do not weep.'" Then He proceeded to raise the young man, and gave him back to his mother.

Pilate washed his hands of Jesus, but Jesus could never wash his hands of Pilate. Even on the road to Calvary Jesus felt sorry, not for himself, but for the deluded people and their offspring.

Christ came to earth to reveal to mankind the life and the character of God. Divine mercy is reflected in the compassion of Christ. Christ never treated multitudes as multitudes. He thought of them as individuals. His bigheartedness could take time and make room for the problems of each individual who came to Him. His heart went out to publicans and sinners, to rich and to poor, and His love and confidence started them off again on the road toward God.

However miserable and disappointing Jesus' disciples were, however much they underestimated and misunderstood Him, He nevertheless continued to associate with them. Although they sometimes proved disloyal to Him, He continued loyal to them. Although their love for Him was flighty and undependable, His love for each was constant and strong. Although their interests were all too selfish and worldly, He gave them the best that He had.

Christ did everything divinely possible to build people up in their most holy faith. Jesus could foresee what people will become when they open their hearts to the Spirit of God. In spite of their weaknesses and faults, He knew that many of them were going to accept the grace of God, and would become saints of earth and of heaven.

Jesus was unique. Often He was lonely. No one really understood Him. In the things that concerned Him most, no one on earth could help Him. One of the saddest moments in His life was the time when He went to Gethsemane. Three disciples followed Him closely, yet none of them was able to speak the word that He needed. How He yearned for the compassionate support of His friends! In His crisis, they all ran away from Him.

On the cross Jesus suffered the bitter pain of complete isolation, even from His heavenly Father. But in that mental agony He was sorry, not for himself, but for the multitudes who would suffer for rejecting their own God-given Savior. Even in suffering He prayed for others, asking God to forgive them.

The mind and heart of Christ are infinitely greater than any human mind and heart, yet He sympathizes with the real needs of each individual. Jesus looked at people until He could see each one as a person of human value and un-

114

told spiritual possibilities. He looked at people in such a way that He could see in each one what no one else had ever seen before. In fact, He saw more in each personality than what the individual himself could see.

BEING CHRIST TO OUR FELLOW MEN

Martin Luther once said, "We must be Christ to our fellow men." We have the rare privilege of carrying on the work of Christ after Him. Ours is the opportunity to do what Christ would do for our fellow men. One of the marvels of life today is to discover and observe Christ at work in and through thousands of His consecrated workers.

People crave sympathy and understanding. They want to be noticed. Is it not the Christians who must take the lead in showing a genuine interest in the real needs of other people? The primary interest of the church should be in persons, rather than in teachings and institutions as such. Our doctrines and missions are the blessed and necessary means for helping people, but they are not ends in themselves. The fundamental aim of Christianity is the spiritual redemption and development of the individual. The purpose of religion is "that the man of God may be complete, equipped for every good work." The aim of Christianity is complete manhood, and the ultimate aim of all is the glory of God.

The new creation imparted to us in baptism, or at conversion, and nourished by the Word of God and the Lord's Supper, should be permitted to find expression in service to our fellow men for Jesus' sake. The finest Christian speech is a Christian life. The best argument for Christianity is a real Christian.

People would rather see a living demonstration of Christianity than to hear about it. People may have difficulty in

115

understanding what we try to tell them, but they can readily understand the gospel as revealed in daily acts of kindness and helpfulness. "That which maketh a man to be desired is his kindness" (American Standard Version). The key that arouses interest and starts many people on the road to God is a realization that somebody is really taking an interest in them.

The whole program of Christ for saving souls depends to a large degree on the individual in the service of Christ. Christ has no other method. Christ is depending on the people in His Kingdom to carry on His work after Him. Christianity has been spread through the personal touch, and that is the only way in which it can be spread, today, or any day. A Christian is constrained by love to share with others the comfort God has given him.

It is the Spirit of Christ in the lives of the Christians that has attracted millions to the Light. The Kingdom of God lives and moves and has its being in the lives of the Christians. The Lord has no other earthly home but in the hearts of His hospitable people. He has no other workshop than the active lives of those who participate in His blessed service.

Only he can win souls for the Kingdom who harbors a deep compassion for people. A winner of souls prays for his friends and acquaintances, and desires to manifest a true compassion in some definite way. Before he speaks with others concerning their welfare, he waits upon God for guidance so that he may deal wisely, not just for their immediate pleasure but for their long-time welfare. Actually, it is God alone who can bring about a conversion and develop the Christian life. Yet God uses people in making contacts with prospective Christians and new converts.

How thankful a person ought to be that there are people on every side whom he may help! The sight of Christian people is indeed cause for deep gratitude. It is "folks" that make our cities, our factories, our farms, our schools, our homes, our churches. It is "folks" that give value to minerals, gems, land, crops, business, ideals, and religion. It is "folks" that give value to friendship. The world would not mean so much to us if there were no other people here.

The Similarity of People

Throughout the world people are much more alike than different. We all have certain common characteristics; and Christians have still more in common. We are more like others than we at first surmise. They have ideals just as we have. They have faults just as we have. Our failings certainly are not intentional. Neither are the failures of fellow Christians. Their advantages are no more valuable than ours.

Each of us has so much for which to be truly thankful. It may be that others are jealous because of the things we enjoy. They crave compassion, friendliness, and understanding, just as we do. When we look down from an airplane or a high building, one person on earth seems about as limited and as blessed as the others.

Arthur W. Robinson has wisely said, "Every man, after all, is a boy, more or less grown up. At times people may be bombastic, at times very quiet; so are we. At times they might be confiding, at other times shiftless and indifferent; so are we. At times they are bold and courageous, at other times timid and fearful; so are we."

It has been said that there is so much good in the worst of us, and so much bad in the best of us, that it is better for none of us to criticize the rest of us. We are part of all that we have met. Something of us likewise goes into the lives of others, further than we realize.

117

What people really need most of all is to get right with God, to find peace with God, and to find God as their ever-present Friend. As Christians, we have the privilege of pointing others to the Lamb of God. People need food, clothing, a home, and so forth, but people's hearts are still unfed, unclothed and homeless, unless we help in some way to bring to them the blessings of the gospel.

Some people seem to imagine that a Christian is "different" from other people. They hesitate to share their problems with him. Sometimes it may be true, as is true with certain business executives and professional men, that a Christian makes himself unapproachable and inaccessible. Yet a Christian ought to be the easiest person to speak with. People ought to find it easy to make contacts with a Christian for a frank and free discussion of anything at all.

Believers in Christ in every land have always been in a class by themselves. Quite often we make distinctions between those who are friendly to church and those who are indifferent. In most churches various officials are installed for their special work. The very feature of joining the church, and possibly being chosen for special work, tends to thrust some people into a class by themselves. Sometimes election or appointment to an office tends to isolate a person from the very people he ought to be serving.

The Christian calling itself creates a separation. A person who is interested in the Kingdom becomes separated from those who are on the "outside." Yet a saved person yearns with true Christian love to help those who have not yet come to the light. Humanly speaking, one who himself has been a seeker for salvation, and found it, ought to be well qualified to help others to seek and to find peace in God.

The Christian cannot be indifferent to the needs of people about him. Some people have lost confidence in Christianity because of the superior and officious and indifferent attitude that some so-called Christians assume toward them. But a true Christian realizes that, if it were not for the grace of God, he himself would be on the outside, looking to someone possibly in vain, for friendliness and counsel.

People want some dependable person to whom they can unburden themselves. We ought to show people the courtesy of listening attentively as they try to relate to us their problems. Just to listen may be sufficient help for many people. This feature of Christian helpfulness is an art which can often be learned only after many years in the school of Christ. To learn the lesson of compassion for our fellow men will save us from the blight of selfishness and arrogance.

Sometimes we hear that young people are to be preferred in places of responsibility in the church, for, it is said, they are still human. They have more life. They have not advanced so far from their own common position. People who say such things do not realize that many older Christians are still quite human and may love their fellow men with a purer love than many young people can show.

As the Christian advances in spiritual and practical attainments he sometimes loses the popular appeal. Others around him may not be able to understand him. He who has found peace in his own soul is likely to become self-satisfied and become indifferent to the needs of others. His attitude toward the Kingdom and toward life may thus become impersonal.

A Christian's growth in grace sometimes leads to heights and depths difficult for the average person to understand. His old friends may or may not have grown with him. He begins to lose patience with them. He grows along his line of thought and activity, and they develop along their line of endeavor. He may study his Bible every week or every day; others may study theirs hardly at all. He may diligently read church papers; others may not even subscribe. A Christian needs to be on guard so that he maintains the common touch.

WE ARE HERE TO HELP OTHERS

If we have belonged to the church over a number of years, the Lord is looking to us to be witnesses for Him. As witnesses, our work will be accomplished in the degree in which we make actual contacts with the hearts of others. We are not in this world to develop ourselves intellectually or materially. We are here to help people to grow spiritually.

We have no purpose in life apart from the people with whom we ought to associate. We do not work because of the work itself, but for the benefit of the people. We do not build a church or an institution for the sake of the building, but to help the members. We do not participate in public worship just to maintain a custom, but to inspire the worshipers. The apostles did not write their gospels and epistles just to be making literature, but to edify the readers. Our Lord and the disciples always spoke the language of the common people.

As the Christian grows he ought to try to take his family and his friends along with him. There is no special joy in finding a blessing for one's own delight unless one shares that blessing with others. The aim should be, not to grow away from fellow Christians toward God, but to help others to grow along with one toward God.

It was the daily life of Paul that convinced many of the truth of the gospel. In spite of Paul's sufferings at the hands of unbelievers in various places, he had a heart of compassion. In his own mind he was determined to speak in love the message that he knew would transform the lives of those

120

who would listen. With the same purpose in mind, we will do everything possible to maintain the common touch. We must press on together toward our common home.

Thank God for the Common People

Throughout the centuries it has been the common people who have brought the gospel to the world. They have been the source of every political, social and religious improvement. Not many great, not many noble are called. God uses ordinary people in His service. Under God, they will continue to be the salt of the earth. The most unlikely people are the very ones who may be the most appreciative and who may profit the most from our attitude of helpfulness. With such people we ought to maintain the most friendly contacts. What better can we do than to love them for Jesus' sake, and our own sake!

In order to gain the ear and the heart of his fellow men, a person ought to show a real interest in them. It is well to become acquainted with the habits and the hobbies of various people. He must be interested in the things in which they are interested. He must know something of their heroes, and something of their religious thinking.

A Christian learns to respect the opinions of others. He keeps posted on their likes and dislikes, and he might well adopt some of their worth-while customs. In their pleasures, as well as in their sorrows, he feels a strong personal interest.

The words "compassion" and "sympathy" mean to "suffer with!" A sympathetic person suffers with the other person; he accepts the other person's trials as his own, and then he proceeds to do something about it. Sympathy is not sympathy until a person actually helps the person in need. A follower of the Lord wants to do to others as Christ would have him do to them.

The rich young man who came to Christ thought more of his possessions than he did of his fellow men. He had no thought except for his own needs and comforts and vanity. Turning his back on the poor, he also turned his back on Christ, and on his own spiritual welfare.

Helping People to Help Themselves

There are many false conceptions of helpfulness. Many people rely altogether too much on others and lack the elements that make true character. People ought, as much as possible, to learn to rely on themselves. Instead of idly envying the good fortune of others, they ought to take pride in their own work. Helping people who can help themselves is unwise charity.

Theodore Roosevelt once said, "Man does owe a duty to his fellow men, but he also remembers that in the long run the only way to help people is to make them help themselves. It is both foolish and wicked to teach the average man who is not well off that some wrong or injustice has been done him, and that he should hope for redress elsewhere than in his own industry, honesty, and intelligence."

It may be utter wickedness to help someone with a direct gift. It may be better to lend him a good book or magazine, or to help him find employment. A true manifestation of compassion includes helping our fellow men to keep their self-respect.

Jesus helped people, not only directly, but more often to help themselves, by offering them opportunities to work in His vineyard, or by enabling them to earn their own living. Then they became strengthened in body, mind, and soul, and were enabled and inspired to go out and make many more disciples for the Lord.

The branches of a grapevine are of no earthly use for fuel,

122

or building material, or for industrial purposes. Their only purpose is to bear fruit—for others. The branches in Christ, the Vine, fulfill their purpose only in so far as they live for others. A Christian has no right to live for himself. He is saved to serve. A Christian institution has no right to exist for its own sake. Its life is justified only as it serves the present and the rising generation and prepares the way for the future.

Christianity not only makes a man a better man but it also relates him to the needs of others everywhere. Christian compassion is nothing but the power of seeing, arousing, and encouraging the best possibilities in one's fellow men.

A person cannot live alone. He cannot play the game of life alone. He cannot thrive in business alone. He is dependent upon others for many things. He lives, and learns, and grows as he makes effective contacts with others. He learns to be thankful for the rich heritage which he has received from others, and he also learns to contribute his full share in order that the lives of others dependent upon him may be as complete and as rich as possible.

It is the Christian's privilege to help bear the burdens of others and so fulfill the law of Christ. The measure of life is the measure of self-sacrifice. The sacrificial life is the fruitful life. We grow by what we do unselfishly for others. It is through man's compassion and helpfulness that God saves a person from his selfishness and greed. We are honored when we are asked to help others with our time, our gifts, or our service. Those who cast their bread upon the waters will find it after many days.

We expect altogether too much from other people, and we usually underestimate the good which we are able to do for them. We indeed are able to do much more for others than we at first imagine. We shall find the meaning and purpose of life when we find something to live for, something outside of ourselves. Life becomes significant when we can find somebody who will be benefited by our labors of love.

It is not enough just to give to charities, so that someone else may work in our place. We need to do some of that work ourselves. In helping others we miraculously help ourselves. Our chief need in life is to get somebody to inspire and encourage us to do what we are able, or will become able, to do.

As time goes on, we begin to learn that life is not a reservoir, but a channel; not a cistern, but a pipe. We are not ends in ourselves, but instruments for aiding others.

Every time we are asked to do something for someone else in need, it is really the Lord who is giving us an opportunity to invest in treasures for ourselves in heaven. We who have a roof over our head, clothes on our back, food on our table, and the simple enjoyments of Christian civilization, are among the most fortunate of human beings. As citizens of a free country, we can be deeply grateful for the privilege of being good neighbors to anyone who might be in need.

A Christian wants to practice generosity, not only in what he gives, but also in what he receives for his labor and products. He who demands full price for everything he does is taking his reward on earth. When he comes to appear before the judgment throne, the Lord will say of him, "He has received his reward." He demanded it on earth; he received it. And there is nothing more for him in glory. Is it not better for people to be modest in their charges, and not to receive everything which they deserve? For them there remains a rich reward by grace in eternity.

A thankful Christian is willing to share the sacrifices of God's people everywhere. Years ago John Wesley wrote

these words in the front of the Bible given him by his
mother, "God first; the other fellow second; and I'm third."
Such a helpful attitude toward life cannot but lead to great
spiritual enrichment.

> *To serve the present age,*
> *My calling to fulfill;*
> *O may it all my pow'rs engage*
> *To do my Master's will.*

CHARLES WESLEY.

Chapter XV

MY NEIGHBOR

WHEN a person yields himself to Christ, his whole attitude to other people is changed and transformed. Instead of using other people to serve himself, he looks at people through the eyes of Christ for the purpose of helping them.

How Christ works through His people is illustrated in an experience of Sundar Singh. Singh was a wealthy young man in India who discovered Christ as his all-sufficient Savior, renounced his old religion, and became a Bible teacher.

One day in northern India, as Sundar Singh was walking down the mountain with a friend, they found a man lying in the snow, freezing. The Saddhu's companion refused to lend a helping hand, fearing that if they took time to linger by the way, all of them would succumb to the bitter cold; so he went on.

Singh, however, picked up the frozen man and carried him on his shoulders toward the next village. As he trudged along carrying his living burden, he himself was warmed and invigorated by his hard labor. The frozen man on his back also was warmed, and came back to consciousness and life. By his spirit of helpfulness, Sundar Singh's own life was spared; but his companion, who had tried to spare himself, was later found frozen to death in the snow.

Tolstoi has beautifully related how Christ comes to answer the plea of the needy, as well as to bless him who

126

serves. Martin was a shoemaker who lived and worked in a basement. Everyone knew that he was an honest workman. His wife and children had died. He was so lonesome that he wanted to die.

As Martin began to think of the salvation of his own soul, a wayfarer suggested that he read the Bible. "God gave you your life," the wayfarer declared. "When you give your life to God, you will find happiness."

Martin purchased a Bible with large type and began to read. One night as he was reading the Scriptures he dozed and it seemed that someone came and whispered into his ear, "Martin, tomorrow I am coming to visit you." Immediately he knew that it was the Lord who was going to come.

Next day Martin hardly dared to work for fear of missing the welcome stranger. A man stopped by the door. At first Martin imagined that it was the Lord, but it was only Stephen who was shoveling the snow away from the doorway. Stephen was weak, and old, and cold. Martin invited him inside and gave him a cup of tea. When that was gone he poured out a second cup, and a third.

After Stephen was gone, there stopped by Martin's doorway a woman with a crying baby in her arms. Both had insufficient clothing for the cold weather. The woman tried to wrap her arms about the screaming baby to keep it warm. Martin went to the door. "Come in, and warm yourself," he said to the shivering mother.

The woman explained that she and the baby had had nothing to eat that day. Martin hurriedly found some bread and warmed some soup. While the mother ate, Martin tried to give the baby some warm milk with a spoon and thoroughly enjoyed himself as he tried to make the baby smile.

The mother explained that she had heard nothing from her husband who had gone to the army a few months previously. She had lost her job, and could find no work. Mar-

127

tin gave her an old coat and a coin. Thankfully the woman went her way.

In the afternoon Martin saw an old woman carrying a bag of chips and shavings and a basket of apples. As she put the heavy bag down to change it to the other shoulder, a boy snatched an apple and started to run off. But the woman caught him by the shoulder, shook him hard, and talked to him roughly. The boy screamed for help.

Martin went out and suggested to the woman that she should forgive the boy, and also told the boy that he should not steal from anybody. He gave the boy an apple and promised the woman that he himself would pay for it. After Martin had spoken to them for a moment about Christian living the woman began to pick up her bag, but the boy said he would carry it for her.

After supper Martin sat by his lamp. He picked up his Bible and opened it. He mused over the dream, or the vision, or whatever it was he had heard or seen the night before. He wondered why the Lord had not come as He had promised. In one corner of the room Martin imagined that he saw some people, but he could not distinguish just who they were.

"Who is it?" inquired Martin. "It is I," said happy Stephen, as he stepped forward and disappeared. "It is I," said the smiling woman with the baby, and disappeared. "It is I," said the old woman and the boy, as they stepped forward and disappeared.

Martin was overjoyed. Then he turned his eyes to the page before him, and read, "For I was hungry and you gave me food, I was thirsty and you gave me drink, I was a stranger and you welcomed me. I was naked and you clothed me . . ." And farther down, "As you did it to one of the least of these my brethren, you did it to me." And so Martin's vision had come true, and in these needy visitors the Savior

128

had really come to him. And the prayers of these people likewise had been answered in the kindness and helpfulness of Martin.

Hull House in Chicago has been a mecca for tens of thousands of needy people. Its founder, Jane Addams, spent the major portion of her life, first in founding, then in enlarging and managing, this important humanitarian venture.

Some two months before her departure Dr. Daniel A. Poling asked Miss Addams, "What is the secret of your life?" Miss Addams replied, "I looked up into the face of Christ, and then I looked into the faces of these boys and girls and I tried to bring them together."

Neighborliness Toward Other Church Groups

In our day there is ample room for a better understanding of the work carried on in all denominations. We know one another all too little. Wherever the Word of God is preached in its truth and purity, there His Spirit is active in the hearts of men.

Too often we judge other groups by their worst representatives, while we flatter ourselves because of our own best representatives. Would it not be better never to judge at all, but rather to try to be sympathetic with the noble purposes and motives of the consecrated members of each church group?

Some years ago in Lansing, Michigan, a speaker gave this illustration from his own life. Someone had asked him to which denomination he belonged. "Well," the speaker replied, "originally I was a Methodist, I suppose because my parents were Methodists. If they had been something else, likely I, too, would have been something else. But I'm a Methodist and I'm glad of it. I love my church in spite of some evident shortcomings common to all.

"For a few years we lived in a community where the Baptist Church was quite close, and I attended the Baptist Sunday School. So I became a kind of Baptist-Methodist.

"Some of our neighbors were Lutherans. They were honest, hard-working people whom I admired. They had something I needed, so I became a kind of Lutheran-Baptist-Methodist.

"As I grew up I happened to visit a Presbyterian Church. There is something about their services that I liked. Many of their people I learned to love. So I became, you might say, a Presbyterian-Lutheran-Baptist-Methodist.

"Interested in the church at large, I came into contact with the Disciples of Christ. I read some excellent books written by Episcopalians. I discovered that many of the hymns in our own hymnal really originated in some other denomination. I visited various institutions of learning, orphans' homes, hospitals, old people's homes, several kinds of institutions, which had been founded and were being supported by all kinds of churches.

"Even from evangelical movements within the medieval church, such as represented by St. Augustine, Savonarola, St. Francis of Assisi, John Huss, and so forth, we all have received a rich heritage.

"One day I happened to attend a service in a Jewish synagogue. The rabbi read one of the Psalms of David. He read from one of the books of Moses; he quoted one of the major prophets. And I thought, Surely, we owe much to God for His work through the Jewish people in many generations. Thousands of Jews in Europe and in America have accepted Christianity.

"I know I am a better Christian because of what I have learned from people in all branches of Christian faith. I tried to reach out and adopt the best from all denominations. Anybody who sincerely loves the Lord Jesus Christ ought to be a good friend of mine. God has brothered all believers in Christ. We are a part of all that we have met. We are members of one another, and all one body in Christ.

"We really belong to all denominations that have helped us. So if you ask me to what denomination I belong I have to answer that I am a Jewish-Catholic-Evangelical-Reformed-United Brethren-Quaker-Disciples of Christ-Episcopalian-Church of God-Congregationalist-Presbyterian-Lutheran-Baptist-Methodist."

Near the rim of a wheel the spokes are spaced some distance apart. But near the hub each spoke comes closer to other spokes, in fact, each spoke is shaped so as to fit and make room for other spokes.

In our usual daily affairs we are often too much detached from other people. But as we come ever closer to Christ, the hub of the universe, we come also closer to other people, especially God's people. In fact, we permit ourselves to be fitted so as to conform, at least in part, with the experiences and attitudes and practices of fellow Christians.

The late premier of Canada, W. L. McKenzie King, once said, "The spiritual interpretation of life teaches us that all human life is sacred; that we are members one of another; that the things which we have in common are greater than those which divide; that each is his brother's keeper."

It is well to be neighborly, but we best serve the highest interests of the Kingdom of God at large by being most zealous and loyal to God's work in our own church. It is said of some people that they are so socially minded that they neglect their own business, their own homes, and their own families. We best serve humanity by tending to our own business. As we labor faithfully in our own section of the Lord's vineyard, we can improve both the quality and the quantity of our own labors by keeping our hearts and eyes open to the work which the Lord is doing in and through other churches as well.

As a young man, St. Francis of Assisi was wealthy. He could have had anything that he desired. But he was not happy. Finding Christ, he began to serve his fellow men, and he confessed that he was never so happy as when he was out with people, speaking with them, and sharing with them the blessings which God had given him. In prayers by St. Francis we observe something of his greatheartedness:

"Lord, make us instruments of Thy peace. Where there is hatred, let us show love; where there is injury, pardon; where there is discord, union; where there is doubt, faith; where there is despair, hope; where there is darkness, light; where there is sadness, joy; for Thy mercy and Thy truth's sake, Amen."

"O Divine Master, grant that I may seek, not so much to be consoled, as to console; to be understood, as to understand; to be loved, as to love. Grant that I may become willing, not to be served, but to serve; not to receive, but to give; For it is in giving that we receive; it is in pardoning that we are pardoned; and it is in dying that we are born into Eternal Life."

132

Chapter XVI

THE MAGNETISM OF JESUS

THREE million Christian martyrs would not have needed to die if they had spoken only one word, a word denying Christ. But realizing the unflinching faithfulness and the willing sacrifice of Christ in dying for them, they prayed for grace to be loyal to Him, even though they should die for their faith. The magnetic pole in the life of millions of Christians throughout the centuries has been Christ. Thus they learned to be dependable in the performance of their duties for Jesus' sake.

The crown of all Christian blessings is grace to be faithful and dependable. In the final day, every person will be judged, not by his outward success, but by the degree in which he has been faithful to the opportunities God has given him. For . . ."it is required of stewards that they be found trustworthy."

If a branch in Christ does not bear fruit, He cuts it off. It was not an avowed enemy, but Judas, one of the disciples, a onetime friend, who betrayed the Lord and entered into the service of the prince of darkness. He knew where his Master might be found. Judas is an outstanding example of the possible unfaithfulness of any follower of the Lord.

The first to make a good confession in Christ as the Son of God was Peter. But Peter was also the one who later denied his Lord three times. In the Garden of Gethsemane all the disciples ran away from Christ. Only John had courage faithfully to remain with his Lord in the trial. All the disciples needed to learn the lesson of faithfulness.

Even though a person may stand high in the family of God, he needs to lean hard on his Lord, lest he listen to siren voices and be led astray from the faith. He who has strayed away, but returns and confesses that he has been an unfaithful servant, may, under God, learn to become the most faithful and dependable of all.

God Is Always Faithful

Christian faithfulness begins with a realization of the faithfulness of God. How unflinchingly and dependably God deals with His whole creation!

"God is faithful, by whom you were called into the fellowship of his Son, Jesus Christ our Lord."

"He is faithful that promised."

"He who calls you is faithful, and he will do it."

"God is faithful, and he will not let you be tempted beyond your strength."

"But the Lord is faithful; he will strengthen you and guard you from evil."

"If we are faithless, he remains faithful."

"He who promised is faithful."

"If we confess our sins, he is faithful and just, and will forgive our sins and cleanse us from all unrighteousness."

Our loyalty to Christ depends upon our sinking ourselves deep into the faithfulness of God. God will not let go. "Underneath are the everlasting arms." At all times God remains a dependable and trustworthy Refuge. He who watches over His people will never slumber nor sleep.

He who has planted in the hearts of His people the seeds of faith is not going to give up very easily His claim on their

134

lives. "He who began a good work in you will bring it to completion at the day of Jesus Christ." God is doing His part. Now it is our privilege to yield to Him, completely and sacrificially.

LOYALTY TO CHRIST

Our faithfulness is something much more vital than loyalty to an institution, a church, or a cause. Our Christian devotion is directed to a Person. We speak of the love of a pupil for a teacher, or of a child for a parent, or of a soldier for his country. But a Christian's loyalty to Christ is much more intense than any of these.

Christ's service for each human soul has been so far-reaching and all-inclusive that we owe much more to Him than to anyone else in all the world. We can serve Him day and night as long as we live, and in eternity, and still we have only begun to show our faithfulness as He deserves to be served. We want to be devoted to Christ, not because we want to merit some favor from Him, but because He has already been abundantly merciful to us.

When we learn what Christ has done for us, we marvel at the mysterious love behind it all. We wonder at the orderliness of all nature, and are concerned at the disorderliness of human life. The elements in the universe are so ordered and fitted together as to be obedient to the laws of the Creator.

"That which God places upon me here and now is part of His great plans for the universe." When a person is disobedient to God everything in nature seems to work against him. But when a person becomes obedient to God everything in nature seems to help and to encourage him. Would it not be remarkable if we could become as equally yielded to the will of God as the elements are?

Our faithfulness to God is a fruit of the Spirit which comes from the faithfulness of God. Loyalty to Christ aims toward harmony with the good and gracious will of a loving God. A faithful person plans to take time for God, to be still before Him, to consult His will, and to wait upon God.

Trustworthiness implies keeping oneself available for the call of God and ready for anything that God needs done in His Kingdom. It also implies a willingness to labor in the background, if need be, in order that the interests of the Kingdom may advance and grow.

As Christians, we have much to learn from the watchfulness of the greedy. How carefully the miser deals with reference to every little profit, or opportunity, or the use of each minute! How carefully he avoids even little disbursements for the sake of his idol! How shrewd he is to gather more, and to keep more for himself! Night and day he occupies his thoughts with his business and submerges personal desires for the sake of his greed. How much more faithful should not a Christian be with reference to the use of the talents God has entrusted to him!

Whatever others say or do, or not say and not do, a Christian determines to be dependable in his Christian duties. We want to be willing to pay the price of faithfulness to our Master. Under the banner of the King of kings it is our privilege to be on-the-job soldiers. "Everything depends on my being faithful; and I depend upon God, who is faithful."

As in showing patriotism, loyalty to the Kingdom of God consists of much more than only singing songs and pledging allegiance. It consists in remaining faithfully at our posts of duty and in paying our tribute at times when less faithful people are shirking their duty. "Not every one who says to me, 'Lord, Lord,' shall enter the kingdom of heaven, but he who does the will of my Father who is in heaven."

Developing One's God-Given Talents

Dependability comprises the beginning, the continuation, and the crown of a proper administration of our Christian life. Talents and capabilities, as well as possibilities for development, both temporal and spiritual, differ greatly.

One person possesses great talents; another person has limited gifts. One person has received five talents; another, two; another, one. The Lord, who is just and righteous in all His ways, does not require the same results from each one. But one thing He does expect of all, and that is trustworthiness in the use of what they do possess.

If the Lord has given any of us only one talent, it is not good to resort to self-pity or envy concerning others. Blessed is he who does not dig the one talent into the earth, but rather employs his limited capability wisely and consistently in the service of the Lord. It was the man who failed to use his one talent who was declared to be wicked and negligent. "Cursed is he who does the work of the Lord negligently."

Time and again the history of the world has proved that it is not always the five-talented people who perform the greatest works for humanity. Often it is the one-talented people who realize their limitations, but who nevertheless apply themselves all the more diligently to make the best possible use and development of what they can do.

The Lord holds us responsible, not only for the talents that He gives us, but also for the improvement and increase which the original talents rightfully ought to produce if we are loyal to Him. And to be faithful to Him implies that we are willing to be weaned away from devotion to lesser things

137

and pray for grace to be truly reliable in the one, important thing needful.

When personal faith is lacking, faithfulness also will be deficient. He who excuses himself, accuses himself. But where there is true faith in God there will also be true faithfulness to Him.

Socrates once said, "Not only is he idle who does nothing, but he is idle who might be better employed." We are not here to have our own way; we are here to go God's way, to get hindrances out of His way, and to go with Him all the way. We have only one thing to do in this life, and that is to be doing the one thing we know God wants us to be doing. Regardless of personal desires the angels of heaven take keen delight in being devoted to God at all costs. This life, an apprenticeship for heaven, is a school where we learn how to be true to God.

"Give me," the prodigal son demanded of his father before he left home. But having left home, finding the other life empty and disappointing, and returning to his father, the humbled son meekly prayed, "Make me." "Treat me as one of your hired servants." We cannot make ourselves faithful servants of God. Only God can make us faithful to himself.

God wants to make of us something more than hired servants. He wants us to be His friends. And still more, He wants us to enjoy the full rights and privileges of redeemed children of His. Such generosity on the part of God attracts us to want to serve Him all the days of our life.

PLACING OURSELVES BEFORE THE FACE OF THE LORD

The genuineness of a Christian's loyalty to God may be discerned by the manner in which he takes care of his own soul. He is most faithful when he mercilessly seeks by the grace of God to place himself squarely before the face of the Lord as though he were already come to Judgment Day.

138

Then in the full light of God's holiness and righteousness he can well discern his own waywardness and perversity.

At the revelation of his own natural indifference, a person will feel like getting down on his knees to beg for mercy from a merciful God. And, receiving such mercy and grace, he will rise and pledge himself to serve such a gracious and forgiving God all the days of his life.

Other people may judge a person by the outward results of his labors and endeavors, by what they call success or failure. But the Lord sees the inner pledges and determinations to be loyal to Him, whether a person is successful or not. In the sight of God, outward success does not presuppose faithfulness; neither does failure presuppose unfaithfulness. Regardless of the outcome, whether we fail or succeed, God only expects that at all times we should be loyal to Him.

True Christian loyalty urges a person to be dependable in the performance of his duties, even in the performance of details in secret, when no one else, except God, may ever know the difference. It presumes an unwavering spirit in dealing with those of low estate, the poor, the ill, those who cannot repay, as well as those with whom it may be no social honor to be acquainted. "Small things are small, but faithfulness in small matters is something great."

Anyone who wants to be a sincere Christian regards nothing as small or unimportant. Everything has value in relation to the whole. A true Christian wants to be on the job in the performance of his duties, not only for the sake of the work he is trying to do, but also for his own sake. A person's reliability has a definite reflex action on his own life and character. Only he who is dependable can become the blessing to his fellow men and to the Kingdom of God that God would like for him to be.

A person who wants to be loyal to Christ is determined to

be zealous in the service of the Lord, regardless of the results, whether he harvests honor or shame, gains or losses in this world. He cares nothing for these as long as he can be devoted to his God. At the command of the Lord, even after fishing "all night and catching nothing," he is willing to launch out into the deep.

Such a person is not satisfied with superficial results. He builds solidly. He works for eternity. He provides for unborn generations. The eternal, for himself and all God's people, is his aim and goal. He strives to secure the "fruit that abides."

Most of the satisfaction and joy in a Christian's life come to him in the secret of his conscience, when he knows that he has performed some good work according to the guidance and with the blessing of God. It costs something to be dependable in the work of the Lord, but it costs infinitely more to neglect it. It is impossible for a just God to give to the unfaithful the blessing He would like to give to all. It would not be upright for Him to do it.

Without a doubt, every newly converted or awakened Christian intends and resolves by the help of God to be reliable. Some become increasingly loyal. As the months and years roll by, some are inclined, however, to become careless and a little less loyal. Such people can be restored only through a confession of their carelessness and a return to their former devotion. Without delay they must return to the first love. Otherwise there is danger of their becoming utterly perverse.

There are some Christians who have begun in the Spirit, but have finished in the flesh. In the beginning they certainly were not hypocrites. For a while they ran well. Then their zeal and loyalty began to lag. Other interests distracted them. Their earnestness and sincerity became lax. They began to "warm their hands" in the company of unbelievers. And finally they fell away from the Lord altogether.

If we study the epistles of Paul to Timothy we observe that Timothy must have been inclined to discouragement and waywardness. Paul wrote to him, "Hence I remind you to rekindle the gift of God that is within you through the laying on of my hands; for God did not give us a spirit of timidity but a spirit of power and love and self-control."

There are some people who become undependable in their duties, they say, because other people do not appreciate their efforts. This charge may often be true, but there may be more than they realize who do appreciate their work. People far and wide in God's Kingdom are dependent on every one's doing his duty. There are countless souls who are faithful, and their faithfulness ought to inspire us all to determined trustworthiness.

We do not perform our work for the sake of the people alone; that is only incidental. We want to be loyal for the sake of Christ. He is the One to whom we are responsible. He is depending on each of us. Whether others see us or not, He sees. Whether other people are thankful or not is their responsibility, not ours. But whether or not we are loyal to Christ is our responsibility and privilege before Him. "The Master praises; what are men?" There may be more people than we realize who are thankful because of our determined faithfulness to Christ.

Just what reason are we going to be able to give which Christ will accept for not being faithful to Him? John the Baptist was loyal to Christ, even though he had to go to jail to prove his loyalty. For twelve years John Bunyan was jailed, but the verdict on judgment day will be that Bunyan was loyal to Christ.

A chaplain went to visit Martin Niemoller as he sat in his cell. "Why are you here?" inquired the chaplain. "Why are you not here?" asked Pastor Niemoller. Niemoller was devoted to Christ, even though he had to go to a concentration camp to prove it.

We are responsible, not for the whole world, but only for the faithful discharge of the definite task entrusted to us. We are not to be concerned about what we shall do next year, or next week, but only for what we need to do today.

We want to pray, not that Christ might give us many things, but that we might give ourselves to Him. There are many problems which confront us day by day, there are many jobs which beckon to us so enticingly at the present moment, but none of these is important enough to keep us from doing the one and only thing we know Christ wants us to be doing here and now.

Whatever our occupation may be, it can be dedicated in some way to the service of God. Whatever our job may be, there do come golden opportunities from time to time when we can say a good word or do something good, for Jesus Christ.

Loyalty to Christ often implies loving that which indifferent people hate and despise. It also calls for our being watchful when others are careless, criminally careless. It challenges one to fight onward, quietly and persistently, on the side of God and love and truth. A faithful soul will keep plodding on, saying a good word here, performing a good deed there, and leaving the results with God.

As followers of the Lord, it is well for us to subordinate our own immediate desires for the future welfare of others. Now is the time for us to rededicate ourselves to the unfinished task. Christ started the good work. Others have developed it and handed it over to us. But much remains to be done. Now is it up to each of us to make the best possible use of the talents which God has entrusted to us, to make whatever improvements we can, and to pass the work

142

on to the rising generation. It is not our work, but Christ's work, for He wishes to use us.

If we fail God, we frustrate His best plans for us all, and Jesus' death upon the cross is of little or no avail for those who will not hear the gospel because we have been negligent. It is when a person finds Christ, or rather is conscious of Christ's finding him, that he is gripped and empowered by a sense of mission. Heaven will be worth our best obedience, our hardest labors, our most prayerful devotion.

Christ has no other way. He challenges each of us to yield himself to His trustworthy, unselfish, far-seeing, uplifting leadership. Others do not care. They cannot care. But Spirit-born and Spirit-enlightened and Spirit-led Christians do care. Like the sunflower, their faces always keep turning toward the Sun of their soul.

Dr. C. P. Harry of Philadelphia, for many years a traveling counselor for Lutheran students in colleges and universities, was once asked how he could work so hard, attend so many meetings, travel so many miles, and yet always be full of radiant joy and eager for more work. His modest reply was, "It is simply the secret of a life dedicated to God."

J. Hudson Taylor once said, "I used to ask God if He would come and help me. Then I asked God if I might come and help him. I ended by asking God to do His own work through me."

Charles G. Trumbull has wisely said, "Christ does not want to be our helper; He wants to be our life. He does not want us to work for Him; He wants us to let Him do His work through us, using us as we use a pencil to write with—better still, using us as one of the fingers of His hand."

One Christian, asked to relate what Christ meant to him, said, "Christ is a Friend who has given me confidence that He would teach me how to do whatever He wanted me to do. Time and again this Friend has stood by me and encouraged me. Day by day He has led me. When I have made mistakes He has not scolded me. When I have gone astray His magnetic love has drawn me back to Him. Night and day He has strengthened me, inspired me, enabled me.

"This Friend has led me to meet and to work with some of the finest people in all the world. He has interested me in the enjoyment of the best literature available, the best of art, the best of music, the best of everything. Why shouldn't I, and why shouldn't we all, show our deep, personal gratitude by permitting Him to use us in His blessed service!"

Two young people settled in a western town, the young husband to be school principal, and the young wife to make a home. To them Christ was vital, and their home soon became a gathering place for those who needed fellowship and understanding.

Then came a virulent epidemic and the young couple, devoting their best to care for the stricken, became ill and died. The whole community mourned their passing. What was the secret of their power and influence? The answer was discovered inscribed within the wedding rings, worn by each. "Each for the other——both for Christ."

A boy was trying desperately to move a heavy stone. His father came along and inquired of his son, "Are you doing your very best?"

"Why sure, dad, I'm doing all I can."

Then the father inquired, "Have you asked me to help you?"

Have we asked God to help us? Are we using all the power available to us in personal Bible study and in prayer? Are we trying to propel the car by pushing on the steering wheel or are we letting the motor propel the car? Have we flipped the little switch of dedication to God so that His power, His light, His warmth, and His message may revitalize us and bless all with whom we come into daily contact?

One evening a certain choir was rehearsing John Stainer's magnificent oratorio, *The Crucifixion*. Everything proceeded as usual until a certain passage called for a hold of eight beats. It was not held out full strength to the end. Tapping his stick on the stand, the director stopped the singers and requested them to sing it again. A second time did not satisfy him. They tried it three times; four times.

The director laid his stick on the stand. For a moment there was breathless silence. Pleadingly the director held out his open hands to his singers and implored them, "Ladies and gentlemen, it is not I who says there should be a hold; it is John Stainer."

It is not only men or women who plead with us to be faithful; it is Christ himself.

Christ "died for all, that those who live might live no longer for themselves but for him who for their sake died and was raised."

Dwight L. Moody recommended, "Give your life to God. He can do more with it than you can."

Dr. Edwin Moll once said, "Be loyal to the Royal in yourself."

> *"Only one life; 'Twill soon be past;*
> *Only what's done for Christ will last."*